ITALIAN
IMMIGRANT
COOKING

ITALIAN
IMMIGRANT
COOKING

BY ELODIA RIGANTE

Food Photography by Nicholas Elias

FIRST VIEW BOOKS
Cobb, California

Published in the United States of America by
First View Books

Distibuted by
First Glance Books
P.O. Box 960
Cobb, CA 95426
Phone: (707) 928-1994
Fax: (707) 928-1995

©1995 by First View Books

Library of Congress
Cataloging-in-Publication data 94-62213
Recipe Author, Elodia Rigante,
Italian Immigrant Cooking
Book #1 of Immigrant Cookbook Series
ISBN 1-885440-02-2

President: Neil Panico
Vice President: Rodney Grisso
Managing Editor: Brenda Phillips
Copy Editors: Rita Gordon Siglain, Bill Siglain
Text Editors: Fred Rohe, Meg McDonnell
Book & Cover Design: Leslie Waltzer
Food Photographer: Nicholas Elias
Food Stylist: Claire Murdoch
Project Coordinator: James Minkin
Cover Photographer: Garry Gross
Illustration: Matt Barna

Special thanks to the following stores and individuals for the use of props and locations:
Biordi, San Francisco, CA, The Purple Sage, Cobb, CA, Red Hen Antiques, Napa, CA, Antiques & Things, Middletown, CA, AnnaTiques, Clearlake, CA, Doreen's Antiques, Lower Lake, CA, Crossroads Antiques, Lower Lake, CA, Tile Craft, San Rafael, CA, Ceramic Tile & Design, San Rafael, CA, Linda & Randy Fung, Louisa & Franco Varo, Madelyn Martinelli, Flora Martinelli, Gary & Julie Bagnani, Vi Allara, Fanchon Amoroso

Black and white photography:
Courtesy of the Museum of
  the City of New York
pages 8 & 9, John Muller, *Bleecker Street*, ca. 1940
page 12, Berenice Abbott, *Cheese Store*, 1937
page 13, Berenice Abbott, *Bread Store*, 1937

Courtesy of the Ellis Island Museum
page 10, above, Ellis Island, ca. 1930
page 10, below, Ellis Island, ca. 1904

Printed in Hong Kong by
Palace Press International.

Second printing August 1995

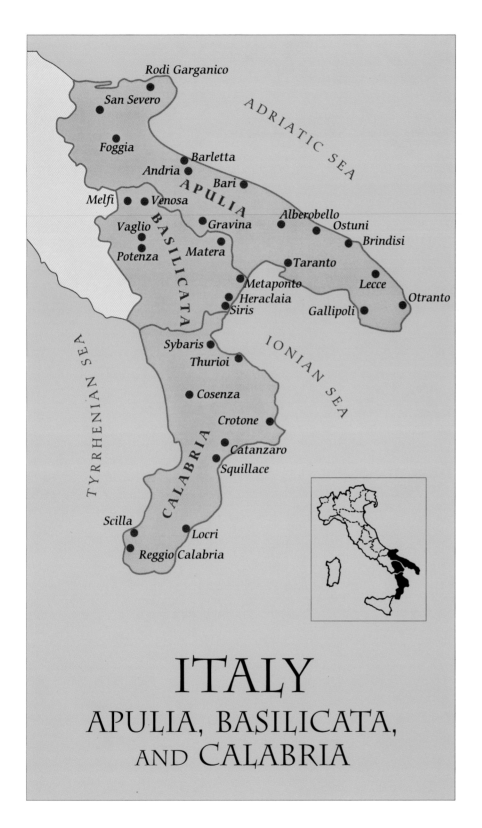

ITALY
APULIA, BASILICATA, AND CALABRIA

DEDICATION

I would like to express my gratitude first to my parents, Rocco and Christina Rigante. Their love and respect for Italy, its culture, and its warm and lively traditions of family and cooking, home and hearth, have always given me and my family so much happiness. And it brings me such joy to have this opportunity to share the richness of their immigrant heritage with others.

I would like to thank all of those terrific people who helped me compile this book. They all worked so hard on it with me, and so enthusiastically. Some of them were already my family —my son Neil, my daughter-in-law Brenda, Neil's friend and business partner Rodney—but having gone through all the stages of the production of this book with all of the others who contributed to it, I now, happily, have a much bigger family than before. And they're all invited to Sunday dinner at my house in New York whenever they can make it!

Special thanks to Barry Moreno, the curator of the Ellis Island Museum, and to the Museum of the City of New York for contributing some Italian-American historical photos. Barry's extensive knowledge of the history of Italian immigrants, and his willingness to pass that on, was very inspirational to all of us.

CONTENTS

FOREWORD
BY NEIL PANICO

Elodia Rigante, my mother, is a virtuoso when it comes to authentic Italian home-cooking. And real Italian cooking is about more than food—it is a way of celebrating the family and sustaining a whole traditional way of life. For my mother, cooking is a great joy. Her cooking certainly has always been a joy for all of those who get to eat her fare. It is also her way of nourishing the values she inherited from the Old Country, and a way that she expresses her love for her family and friends in America, the new world she grew up in.

Of course, I wasn't aware of all of that when I was growing up. I just knew that my family spent many hours every week sitting around the table in her kitchen, talking, laughing, swapping stories—while she piled our plates high with delicious food. Her kitchen was always filled with the people she loved—because she loved to feed the people she cared about. And she still does.

Elodia has an unending enthusiasm for cooking. You just can't get her to stop. And who would want to? She fed me and everyone in our family in the old Italian tradition, just as her mother fed her and her mother had before her. In fact, Elodia comes from a family that has always loved to eat, a family that prides itself on cooking the best Italian food there is.

Elodia's parents, my grandparents, Rocco and Christina Rigante ("Poppanon" and "Mammanon"), came to America in the early 1900s. They bought a delicatessen in "Little Italy" in Brooklyn, and that is how they made their living in the new world. For nearly forty years they lived in an apartment a couple of blocks from their deli—and I grew up only a few blocks from there, myself.

I remember the deli like I was there just yesterday. There were rounds of cheese hanging from the ceiling, just arrived from the Old Country, and olives and hams and sausages, all made in the traditional way—plus the fresh foods my grandparents would make right there on the premises. The whole place was filled with the feeling of Italy, and with smells so aromatic and so fantastic I have never forgotten them. But even more vividly, I remember Sunday dinners in my grandparents' apartment. Those Sunday dinners epitomized the love of family and friends and the passion for excellent food that is the heart of my family's cooking.

When I was growing up, during the 1940s and 50s, it was customary for the younger generation of American-born Italians to go to their parents' home for dinner on Sundays. For my parents (who also took me and my sisters), that meant going to Poppanon and Mammanon's. During those dinners, there was always a lot of talk, and a lot of laughter. Many important matters were discussed, usually with a great amount of passion! Much of the conversation took place in Italian—and I watched the old-timers tell jokes and laugh until they cried. Or, sometimes, they would talk politics, getting louder and louder and poking the air with their hands for emphasis! Or, at other times, they might discuss the latest operetta playing at the neighborhood theatre, or the latest opera recording they had listened to. They would talk about work, about food, about the family. Those weekly get-togethers served an important cultural purpose in our lives—the family bonds were kept tight. But the fantastic meals were a very important part of it, and still are today.

We entered my grandparents' apartment via the kitchen—a huge kitchen that was always full of warmth. It had a big table (It had to be big to hold all the food Mammanon would produce!) and lots of chairs (so that there was always room for friends and for everyone in the family). There, every Sunday, I would see Mammanon cooking the wonderful dishes that she taught my mother to make and that my mother in turn made for me and my family. To me, this book is more than a cookbook—it is a part of our Italian family heritage.

My grandmother, Mammanon, was a bundle of energy, a real dynamo. She attended the 6 A.M. Catholic Mass in her neighborhood every day, no matter what the weather. Then she made breakfast for Poppanon. After that, she opened the deli that she and Poppanon ran. For the rest of the day, she never slowed down. She spent every day importing exotic cheeses, olives, and wines from the country where she was born, preparing traditional foods for the deli the way she learned when she was a girl, selling just the right food items to her friends and customers, cooking for her children and her grandchildren.

Whenever I went to my grandparents' house, I kissed Mammanon hello. It was easy to find her—she was always standing by the stove, cooking. Her long hair was always piled on top of her head, in classic Italian style, and she was always wearing an apron. She was also inevitably wearing black—

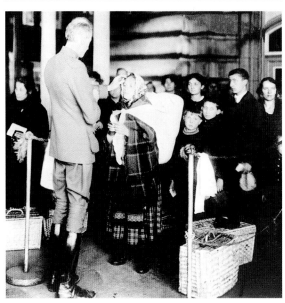

Photos of Ellis Island in New York, the immigration station where Poppanon and Mammanon both first landed in the United States. Ellis Island was opened in 1892, and many of the Italian immigrants who came to this country in my parents' day came through here—in those days, 72% of all the immigrants who came to this country came through this one place.

because somebody in Italy had just died! And there were always candles burning in front of the small religious icons and pictures that she kept scattered throughout her apartment.

When I was a little older, I teased her. Sometimes I swept her off her feet in one of those 1940s romantic dips, telling her what a knockout she was.

"Rocco, Rocco!" she yelled out to my grandfather as I held her over my knee.

"If you weren't my grandmother," I told her, "I'd marry you!"

"Oh, Madonna Mia, discratsia!" she would call out, pretending to be disgraced. She loved playing the game.

My grandfather would be sitting in the living room reading the Italian Sunday newspaper, smoking his Di Nobli cigar, and listening to opera on the Italian radio station or playing Enrico Caruso records on his big old phonograph. He'd just grunt and say something like "dooza botz." (Translation: "The kid is crazy.")

Then I went into the living room to kiss him. I always did, until one time. When I was about twenty-one, I came in but I didn't kiss him. He asked me, "What's the matter, you're too old to kiss your grandfather now? You're a big man or something?" He got the message across—I never stopped kissing him hello until his dying day. And neither did anyone else in the family. That was how it was with Poppanon and his family.

The cooking for Sunday dinner started early in the morning; sometimes, it even started the day before, on Saturday. To describe Mammanon's meals as "bountiful" definitely understates the case. We sat down to eat at about three in the afternoon, and we finished the last course at around seven in the evening. To many, the antipasti, or appetizers, alone would not only be a meal, it would be a big meal—stuffed mushrooms and artichokes, cheeses, olives, roasted peppers, assorted meats, assorted vegetables (stuffed, breaded, sautéed, marinated), and crusty bread. Then came soup, followed by a pasta dish. And then on to the main course—fish or meat, perhaps a stuffed chicken or a meat pie, and vegetables. Salad was next, then dessert and coffee.

But dessert was not the finale. At the very last came fruit and nuts. The men took little knives out of their suit or vest pockets and they peeled their fruit while sipping anisette. Throughout the meal, there was always plenty of homemade wine on the table.

Poppanon made the wine—rich, almost black, heavy, and delicious. The old-timers, the ones who had immigrated to America from the Old Country, were always swapping wines. So, for example, Poppanon would put a jug of wine on the table and say, "Guilano down the street sent this. I gave him one of mine, he gave me one of his. His is pretty good." Of course, that was a cue for the rest of us. "Good, yes. But not as good as yours, Rocco," someone had to say. And he smiled, but, of course, he had to say, "Well, yes. But, you know, Guilano makes a good wine."

After the meal, the music started. Mr. Frank, a neighbor and a friend of Poppanon's, would pull out his mandolin. And everyone would join in singing Italian songs. It could go on for hours. Sometimes, I harmonized with my father, or Poppanon, sometimes we would all sing together. Sometimes, Louise,

Mammanon's brother Dominic in the Fire Brigade in Naples. The potted herbs around him remind me of how important fresh foods were in the cooking Mammanon learned in the Old Country, and how important they are in the cooking that she passed on to me.

another neighbor and good friend of my grandparents, would sing solo. She was beautiful and big-chested, with bright red hair, and she had the most exquisite operatic soprano voice. We all loved to listen to her sing the opera classics in Italian—her voice sent shivers up our spines, it was so good! And that is how our Sunday dinners ended.

Poppanon and Mammanon were both born in Apulia, the heel of Italy's "boot," just south of Naples. It is a region with ancient roots—it was once colonized by Greeks. Today, both Neapolitan and Greek influences still mingle there, and some of the characteristic regional dishes that Mammanon learned while she was growing up in Apulia can be traced back more than a thousand years.

Apulia is a real cornucopia for Italian cooks: table grapes, figs, almonds, melons, citrus fruits, potatoes, eggplant, artichokes, celery, fennel, peppers, and beans are all featured crops. Apulia is also known for its long coastline, the longest in all of Italy. So it is natural that fish and shellfish would appear as often as they do in the Apulian cuisine that Poppanon and Mammanon brought with them. In fact, meat was never a dominant factor in Mammanon's cooking, nor in my mother's. So, although meat dishes appear here and there, they are not a dominant presence in this book. But there is more than one reason for this: as you can tell from the description above, Apulia was populated primarily by farming people—and, as a simple matter of economics, most people from that region could not afford to eat meat frequently.

In our family, we never ate meat on Wednesdays or Fridays. Often, meat would be cooked only once during the week, during the big family feast on Sunday (see pages 148–149). After the Sunday spread, the leftover meats were used in the preparation of pasta and vegetable dishes throughout the

This picture was taken about 76 years ago, when my cousin Angelo had just arrived from Italy. He had a hard time finding a job in the U.S., but at one place they told him if he had a family, they would give him a job. So he had this photo taken with me and my brother. (That's me in the middle.) He went back with the photo of his "family," and he got the job. Those were tough years for Italian immigrants.

week. These pasta and vegetable dishes are such a big part of my mother's and my grandmother's cooking that if you prepare them with vegetable stock instead of beef or chicken stock, the recipes in this book can easily provide you with a delicious vegetarian cuisine.

While Sundays and holidays were the occasion for enormous and elaborate meals, eating during the rest of the week was usually the essence of simplicity. When my grandparents' friends sat down with them in the back of their deli, they were often offered slices of fresh Mozzarella cheese, served with virgin olive oil, salt and pepper, fresh Italian bread, sliced tomatoes (if they were in season), and a glass of homemade wine.

Poppanon made the Mozzarella they sold in the deli—it was always fresh and delicious. When I lived with them for a couple of years during World War II, he was still cooking it on an old coal stove in the back room of the deli. I spent many a day back there watching Poppanon as he made the Mozzarella from scratch. By then, his hands were gnarled from years of making the cheese in big tubs of scalding water. When I was younger, he took the time from his busy work day to shape little animals, like bears and dogs, out of the hot Mozzarella for me, and I would eat them as soon as they cooled. I really loved that, but it wasn't just the cheese that I loved—it was the feeling of being with him, and of the Italian tradition he was part of.

Poppanon came to the United States in 1904, and Mammanon came later. Since Foggia, the town she came from,

Berenice Abbott took this photo of a typical Italian deli in New York's "Little Italy." These delis are a big part of how Italians cook and eat—where else are you going to find the wonderful meats and cheeses you can see in the window?

is less than one hundred miles from Bari, the town that Poppanon came from, and since Foggia and Bari are both parts of the same region (Apulia), their families knew one another. When Mammanon came to America, the two families in Apulia asked other cousins, already in America, to play matchmaker. So Poppanon and Mammanon were introduced to one another in "Little Italy," in America, and the transatlantic matchmaking worked!

Mammanon was already an expert in the Italian way of cooking, taught by her own family and by nuns in the convent where she was partially raised. As much as she could, she held to the old ways, even in the new country. And she passed her legacy on to my mother, Elodia. Elodia has told me many times of Mammanon's teaching method: "She told me 'Watch. Watch. Look, learn, and remember.' That was the way she was taught— to remember what she saw, until she could do it, too. And that is how she taught me."

My mother was a good student—she absorbed Mammanon's wisdom about cooking in the traditional way. But Elodia faced another challenge, too: how to take the best of the old ways Mammanon passed on to her and make them work in the new world that she, Elodia, was growing up in. That is what makes her cooking unique: Immigrant cooking has to blend the style of cooking found in the Old Country with the life-style of the New. Throughout this book, you will see Elodia's notes about the types of ingredients common in America and how she incorporated these new ingredients into her cooking, her tips on how to make the traditional dishes in less time due to the fast-paced environment we live in today, and tips on how to preserve the freshness and quality of the traditional dishes in the midst of it all.

Many of the dishes my mother made could also do double duty: We used the leftovers to make fantastic sandwiches for our lunches. Giambotte (see page 99) is one of our family favorites to use this way, as well as Roasted Peppers (see page 18) and many of the egg and vegetable dishes in this book. In fact, the creative use of leftovers has been a key ingredient in my mother's cooking style.

Truly, Elodia's kitchen is the embodiment of her philosophy: "You have to love to cook. The food won't taste good if you don't love to cook." One of my sisters once said to her, "Mom, do you ever get tired of cooking?" You could tell by the look on her face that the thought had never crossed her mind. She pondered my sister's question for a moment, then she answered, "No, there's nothing I like more than cooking."

Elodia's love of cooking good Italian food is demonstrated by the way she eats to this day. Now, she is a single senior citizen, but she very seldom eats canned or frozen entrees—she eats the same dishes she has been eating all her life. "It's healthy, it's delicious, and I like doing it. Why would I do anything else? Who could show me a better way to eat?"

When I was growing up, I don't remember Mammanon or Elodia mentioning health principles when they talked

Another Berenice Abbott photo--this time of a typical Italian bakery. Notice the price of a loaf of bread in those good old days!

about food. They had no formal education to guide them in preparing foods that promote longevity and well-being. They didn't know from reading books that maximizing fresh vegetables and herbs is good. They didn't need to—health-giving qualities are inherent in the methods Mammanon absorbed in Italy and that she taught my mother, Elodia, in America. And the hardy, long-lived people of Apulia are testimony to the life-giving quality of the foods my family has always loved to eat.

Much later in life, though, Elodia did learn the principles of a healthy diet. It became important to her to maintain her health as she aged. Now, in her seventies, she claims, "I'm healthy. And you want to know why? It's because of the way I cooked and ate all my life." She's proud of that—and she has a right to be. If you analyze her cooking, you see that it is fundamentally healthy. Her cooking is generally devoid of artificial or de-natured foods, and it emphasizes fresh, high-quality vegetables, seafoods, and other ingredients that naturally provide what we need for good health—not because she had to think about it, but because that's the way it's always been in the family, in Apulia.

But I do remember that Mammanon and Elodia sometimes discussed the medicinal effects of the herbs they used in their cooking. Elodia told me many times, "When I was growing up, Mammanon never bought medicines. They came from the kitchen. If you cook right and eat right, you can quit making trips to the drugstore. The way we cook, things like garlic, bay leaves, escarole, and vinegar are not just for taste. They keep you healthy."

I was very fortunate to grow up the way I did —nourished by Elodia's love and her good cooking. But it is only now, having left our neighborhood in Brooklyn's Little Italy over forty years ago, that I can fully appreciate Elodia's exceptional talent. I have traveled all over the world and I have enjoyed the world's great cuisines in the finest of restaurants. And I have learned, through many years of experience, that nothing compares to the delicious, fresh, aromatic, home-cooked foods prepared by Elodia and Mammanon.

The recipes in this book are unique to Elodia and Mammanon's wonderful style of home-cooking, and they stem from the ancient tradition passed down in the Italian countryside for many generations, crossing from the Old World into the New.

When I realized how unique my mother's talents are, I encouraged her to share her legacy in the form of this cookbook. Right away, she responded enthusiastically. After all, Elodia Rigante is the woman who has told me dozens of times, "If you want to eat Italian, you have to cook Italian—and you have to cook Italian right!"

INTRODUCTION

I was born in 1916 in Manhattan, New York, on Mulberry Street. Then, my neighborhood was known as "Little Italy"—and it still is. The day I was born, the snow was so high in New York that my father, Poppanon, used to tease me, "The day you were born, the end of the earth came!" He was from southern Italy, and snow was a new thing to him!

We had a big, happy Italian family—I had many older brothers and an older sister who was my "little mother" because she used to help take care of me. But life isn't always easy—and in 1920, when I was three years old, a flu epidemic devastated our home. In four months, we had four funerals. When it was over, my brother Jimmy and I were the only children left. Just like that.

My father was more than a wonderful man—how can I say it?

My father Rocco, or Poppanon, and my mother Christina, or Mammanon. They taught me all I know about great Italian cooking.

He was my pride. During that difficult time, when he had so much tragedy, he held the family together. But when my mother was too ill and couldn't take care of us anymore, he had to put my brother Jimmy and me in a Catholic orphanage, Mount Loretto, for a while. Fortunately, it was a good place. The nuns there were kind to us. And, while Jimmy and I were staying there, I got the first lesson I remember about how to cook with love.

It was my father who taught me. He was totally dedicated to our family, and to Jimmy and me. He worked hard all week, just to make ends meet—like so many Italian immigrants did then. Every Saturday, when he didn't have to work at his job, he cooked for us—he cooked chicken, meatballs, pasta, Italian cookies, all the foods we liked. Then, every Sunday, saint that he was, he went first to visit the cemetery. After that, he came to see Jimmy and me. And he brought the food he made.

We had a wonderful feast with him every weekend—either out on the orphanage lawns or, if the weather wasn't good, in a small kitchen in one of the buildings there. I always felt how much our "Poppanon" loved us and I could see with my eyes how much he loved feeding us. So, yes, he brought the food he cooked for us and he gave us his love—but they were not two different things. They were the same.

Of course, the other person who taught me about how to cook with love was my mother, "Mammanon." She was from Apulia, just like Poppanon. (In fact, she first came to America so she could support her younger brothers and sisters in Italy.) She was a very well-educated Italian, a school teacher, and she had a great wealth of knowledge about traditional Italian cooking. It seems to me she knew everything about cooking and the home, from A to Z.

She had learned to make so many things by hand. Poppanon had another job in addition to the deli, working outside in the cold. (Coming from sunny southern Italy, the cold weather in New York was not easy for him.) She made all his clothes by hand, warm sweaters, gloves, hats, even socks and long underwear! She sewed all our clothes, even our coats, and she knitted beautiful dresses for me, with ruffles and so on. When my own children were born, she did the same for her grandchildren.

When I was growing up, after my time in the orphanage, I noticed that she was the best in the neighborhood at learning new things, and she taught everyone else what she had learned.

It was fortunate for me that she was as good a teacher as she was a cook. From her, I learned most of what I know about cooking. Making pasta by hand, making delicious sauces, hearty casseroles, healing soups, wonderful desserts, making every kind of dish you can imagine—I saw her do it all many times, until I knew how to do it too.

But to me, being in the kitchen with her was more than just learning about cooking. She poured out her energy to me and to all of us, all the time, through her cooking, and through everything she did for us.

Mammanon made me so proud—instead of tiring her, all that she did for us seemed to give her more energy. I'm sure she had her unhappy moments, but I never saw it. All I can remember is how lively, humorous, and full of love for me and for all of us she was. And how full of the love of cooking.

Working with her in the kitchen, I learned over and over again about the connection between food and love, and about how to love my family through the food that I cook for them. It was lucky for all of us that she loved to cook so much and that she was so good at it, but it was particularly good for Poppanon—because he really loved to eat! Even though he knew how to cook too, that is how it worked between them—she did the cooking and he did the eating. And both were happy about it.

Remembering both of them, Poppanon and his love for good food and Mammanon and her love for cooking, is what convinced me that it was a good idea to put this book together (even though I never dreamed how much work it would be!). It wasn't just all the delicious food they taught me to cook that inspired me—it was the spirit behind all their cooking. And that, along with all the practical tips you'll find in these recipes, is what I want to pass on to you.

Recently my own granddaughter asked me, "Grandma, why does your food always taste so good? Do you put something special in it?"

"Yes," I told her, "I put love in it. When I'm cooking, I remember and love the people I'm cooking for. That's why the food tastes so good." In old Italy, they call the secret ingredient "the hand of the cook." It's the hand of the cook that expresses the heart.

Above: Now, in this photo, it's 1992. From left to right, that's my daughter Annette, me, Neil, and my daughter Marilyn. We're on our way to my nephew Vincent's wedding.

Below: This is a photo taken by my son's wife of another Italian deli—this one is right up the street from where I live in Brooklyn's "Little Italy." I do a lot of my shopping here.

ANTIPASTI
APPETIZERS

When my daughter-in-law, Brenda, came to eat at my house for the first time, I started the meal by bringing out the antipasti, like I always do. She was really impressed with the authentic Italian flavor of all the foods I served, and she enjoyed the feeling of our big Italian family. We shared stories, talked and laughed, drank a little wine, and ate. But my poor daughter-in-law didn't realize that the antipasti were just appetizers. When the antipasti dishes were cleared away, she thought that the meal was finished. She couldn't believe it when I started to bring out the soup, the pasta, and the main courses! Antipasti (if you are talking about more than one dish) or antipasto (if you talking about just one dish) means "before the pasta." So, when you serve this course, be sure to let your guests know that there is a lot more to come!

Antipasti can include various types of salami, prosciutto (Italian ham), cheeses such as Provolone and fresh Mozzarella, stuffed vegetables, marinated vegetables such as artichoke hearts, asparagus, and cauliflower, any number of seasonal fresh vegetables such as sliced tomatoes, green beans, or sweet peas, deliciously prepared vegetables such as baked eggplant, roasted peppers, stuffed mushrooms, peperoncini and many varieties of olives, seafood such as clams, mussels, oysters, shrimp, and crab served raw in their shells, steamed, smoked, or as seafood salad, crab cakes, or shrimp balls, among others, and of course Italian bread, always fresh and crusty.

So, yes, my daugther-in-law wasn't all wrong—antipasti can be a whole meal sometimes. And the opposite is also true— quite a few recipes from the other sections of this book can double as antipasti dishes. For example, the prawns wrapped in pancetta from the seafood section, the vegetable frittata from the eggs and vegetable section, or the stuffed rice balls from the pasta and rice section, among many others.

With so much to choose from, how do you decide what to serve? I decide on the assortment based on several factors. First of all, who's coming for dinner? The first time your future daughter-in-law's parents come—that would have to be a big show. The second factor is what is fresh and attractive at the market? Always look for the freshest ingredients. To this day, my son Neil's favorite light meal is an assortment of antipasti—olives, fresh Mozzarella cheese, and vine-ripened tomato slices sprinkled with olive oil, fresh basil, salt, and pepper, a fresh loaf of Italian bread, and a nice Italian wine. Light, nourishing, and nothing could be easier or faster to prepare!

The last factor to help you decide what to serve for your antipasti is based on what your main course is going to be. The main course is important—for instance, I never serve cheese with a seafood meal. My mother, Mammanon, always said that it isn't good for your stomach to mix the two. She was a tiny woman, but she had enough energy to light up the Statue of Liberty. So, obviously, her many health rules about cooking worked for her, and I found that they worked for the rest of the family, too.

To serve the antipasti, arrange it on big platters so that it looks beautiful. Then, when everyone first sits down at the table for dinner, bring your antipasti platter out and put it right in the center of the table. That way, everyone can help themselves to whatever they want. One other thing—when serving antipasti, don't put "dry" foods with "wet," unless you have a platter with compartments that will keep them separate. You don't want the tastes of the different antipasti to run together—you want the flavor of each food to be distinct and delicious each time you taste it!

ROASTED PEPPERS

12 bell peppers
  (use about 3 red to 1 green)
1/2 cup minced garlic
1/2 cup chopped parsley
1/2 teaspoon salt
1/8 teaspoon pepper
1/2 cup olive oil

For garlic lovers, this dish is a slice of heaven and has always been one of my family's favorite antipasto dishes. The peppers do take some time to prepare, but if you make a big batch and keep them in your refrigerator, they actually get tastier as the days go by. Red peppers are the best to use in this dish because they're sweet— but put some green peppers in for color. For extra color, add a few yellow peppers when they are available.

Preheat the oven to 350°F.

Rinse out a large roasting pan, and leave the moisture in the pan. Wash the peppers, and leave the moisture on them. Lay them next to each other in the pan. Lower the oven to 325°F. Bake the peppers until they are soft, anywhere from 30 to 60 minutes, depending on the color of the peppers. (Green peppers take longer to bake than red because their skins are tougher.) Turn the peppers over about half-way through the baking time. When you see that the skins are puffing up a little bit, the peppers are done. Transfer them immediately to a brown paper bag. Sealing them inside the paper bag will make them sweat, which will loosen their skins.

When the peppers are cooled, remove them, one at a time, from the bag. Peel the skins off and discard the seeds. Slice the peppers into thin, julienne strips and place them in a large bowl. (The peppers should be soft but not mushy or you've baked them too long.) Add the remaining ingredients and mix well.

Cover the bowl and marinate in the refrigerater a few hours or longer. (The longer this dish marinates, the better it gets.) Serve the peppers in your antipasti, salads, and even on pizza. These peppers also make a delicious sandwich: Take slices of fresh Italian bread, a thick layer of the peppers, a slice or two of tomato, some lettuce, and serve with a few olives and peperoncini (pickled hot chili peppers) on the side. Because of the olive oil in the roasted peppers, you won't need any mayonnaise.

Makes about 6 cups.

That's me—at "sweet" sixteen.

STUFFED ARTICHOKES

6 large artichokes

2 ½ cups Italian bread crumbs, seasoned

2 eggs

¾ cup grated Romano cheese

¼ cup minced fresh parsley

⅛ cup minced garlic

½ cup + 1 tablespoon olive oil

½ teaspoon pepper

Salt to taste (optional)

My mother used to bake her stuffed artichokes. Cooking them on top of the stove, however, works just as well. But if you choose to bake the artichokes, be sure to cover them or the leaves will get too crispy.

Wash the artichokes well in a cold salt-water bath. Cut off the stems and slice off a thin layer from the bottom of each artichoke. Lightly cut or sear each artichoke bottom crosswise. This allows the juices to penetrate the artichokes from the bottom of the pan. With a sharp knife or kitchen shears, cut off the pointy tips around each artichoke, as well as the very top (about 3/4 inch down each artichoke, depending on the size). Spread the leaves apart like a flower. Set aside.

In a medium-size mixing bowl, combine the bread crumbs with the eggs, cheese, parsley, garlic, 1/2 cup of the olive oil, the pepper, and the salt, if desired. (I try not to put too much salt in my cooking—it's better for you.) The stuffing should be crumbly, not sticky. Loosely stuff each artichoke up to the top with some of the stuffing, taking care not to overload them. The artichokes should still look like flowers, even when the leaves are stuffed.

Fill a large pot with about 1 inch of water, and add in the remaining tablespoon of olive oil. Stand the artichokes in the pan. (Be sure not to get any water on the stuffing—this will make it too sticky.) Bring the water to a boil, cover tightly, then bring down to a simmer. (If you bake the artichokes, place in a covered baking dish, and put in a pre-heated, 350°F oven.) Depending on the size and thickness of the artichokes, the cooking time will be anywhere from 30 to 60 minutes, whether they are steamed on top of the stove or baked in the oven. Test a leaf periodically to see if the artichokes are tender. Serve while hot as an appetizer or as a vegetable side dish.

Serves 4 to 6.

STUFFED MUSHROOMS

2 pounds medium-size mushrooms

2 ½ cups Italian bread crumbs, seasoned

2 eggs

¾ cup grated Romano cheese

¼ cup chopped parsley

½ cup olive oil

½ teaspoon pepper

⅛ cup minced garlic

Salt to taste (optional)

Optional Stuffing Ingredients: salami, prosciutto, Mozzarella cheese, Provolone cheese, peperoni

This dish is a favorite in our home, and can easily be varied for special occasions or holidays by adding any of the optional stuffing ingredients. You might also want to make a large batch of the stuffing to keep on hand for future dishes. It keeps well when wrapped tightly and refrigerated.

Preheat the oven to 350°F.

Wash the mushrooms in a bath of salted cold water. This is Mammanon's method for making the mushrooms "come nice and white." Remove and discard the stems (I always slice and save them for the marinated vegetables in my antipasto), and set the mushrooms aside to drain.

In a medium-size mixing bowl, combine the rest of the ingredients. The stuffing should be loose, not too sticky. Mince any of the optional stuffing ingredients into the stuffing. Adding any of these will create a completely different and delicious mushroom dish.

Put about 1/4 cup of water (very little!) mixed with a teaspoon of olive oil in the bottom of a large baking dish. Stuff the mushrooms and lay them next to each other in the dish. Be careful not to get any water from the pan on the stuffing because this will make the stuffing sticky. Bake uncovered for about 30 minutes.

Serves 6.

GABOLADIN

ITALIAN RATATOUILLE

2 large eggplants

$\frac{1}{2}$ cup olive oil

1 large onion, diced

3 large stalks celery, diced

2 large green or red bell peppers,
   diced

4 cups peeled & chopped tomatoes

1 cup sliced green olives

$\frac{1}{2}$ cup sliced Calamata
   or Italian olives

2 tablespoons capers, drained

2 tablespoons minced garlic

$\frac{1}{2}$ cup red wine vinegar

1 teaspoon oregano

2 tablespoons sugar

$\frac{1}{2}$ teaspoon salt

$\frac{1}{4}$ teaspoon pepper

Some of my Italian neighbors call this dish "caponata," but my family has always called it "gaboladin." Try this popular dish in your antipasto, served with some sliced Italian bread, or as a main course, along with some rice or pasta. My family likes to make a sandwich with it as well. However you eat it, serve this dish either hot or at room temperature, never cold, to fully taste all the flavors.

Wash the eggplants and cut them in half lengthwise. Sprinkle them with a bit of salt and place them upside down in a colander to drain for 30 to 45 minutes. (Salt helps remove acid from eggplant.)

Heat the oil in a large saucepan and sauté the onion, celery, and green or red peppers over low heat until tender. Cube the eggplants (do not peel them—there are vitamins in the eggplant peel), and add to the pan. Add the remaining ingredients.

Cover tightly, and simmer over very low heat, about 45 minutes, stirring regularly. Serve immediately as a main dish, or cover, cool, and let marinate in the refrigerator for several hours (overnight is preferable), then serve at room temperature as an appetizer or sandwich. *Serves 4.*

POLENTA ALLA PIZZAIOLA
POLENTA MARINARA

1 recipe Marinara Sauce
  (see page 164)
1 12-ounce can tomato paste
8 cups water
2 tablespoons salt
1 pound polenta meal or
  coarse cornmeal
1 cup grated Romano cheese
1 pound shredded Mozzarella
  cheese

Mammanon made many dishes using polenta, but this dish was always our favorite. It's excellent as an appetizer or antipasto but also works well as a main course.

Prepare the sauce. For this recipe, you use a thick marinara, so add the tomato paste and let a lot of the moisture evaporate while cooking. Season to taste. You'll need to cook the sauce a little longer than usual.

Bring the water to a boil in a large saucepan, and dissolve the salt. Stirring continuously with a whisk, slowly add the polenta meal or cornmeal. If you are using the coarser cornmeal, you may need to add extra water.

When all the polenta is blended with the water, lower the heat and simmer for approximately 45 minutes, stirring occasionally with the whisk. Then as the polenta begins to thicken, stir instead with a wooden spoon. When the polenta is done, it will come away from the sides of the pan cleanly and be very firm.

Rinse a large glass baking dish with cold water and spread the hot polenta evenly into the dish. Put it in the refrigerator to cool and harden for about 2 hours.

Preheat the oven to 350°F.

Lightly oil a large, oblong baking dish with olive oil. Loosen the sides of the molded polenta from the pan and turn out onto a chopping board. Slice the polenta into 1/2-inch slices. Spread a layer of the polenta slices in the bottom of the baking dish and cover with Marinara Sauce. Sprinkle Romano on top, and then add some of the shredded Mozzarella cheese. Add another layer of the polenta slices, and keep layering the above ingredients until the baking dish is full. The top layer should be polenta drizzled with sauce, covered with some Mozzarella cheese.

Bake for 30 minutes, making sure not to burn the Mozzarella on top. Cool slightly before serving to let the dish settle. Slice and serve hot. *Serves 6 to 8.*

FINOCCHI DORATI
BATTER-FRIED FENNEL

3 fennel bulbs
2 eggs
3 tablespoons flour
1/2 cup milk
1 teaspoon salt
1/2 teaspoon pepper
Olive oil (for frying)

In Italian, the name of this dish means "golden fennel." And that's exactly what it is—golden and delicious!

Wash the fennel well, removing and discarding all the leaves. Steam until tender but still somewhat firm, about 10 minutes. Transfer to paper towels to drain and cool. Cut into 1-inch strips.

In a small mixing bowl, beat the eggs, flour, milk, salt, and pepper. Heat the olive oil in a large skillet until it is hot. Dip each fennel piece in the batter, completely coating it, then fry in the olive oil until golden brown. Drain and cool on paper towels. Adjust salt to taste and serve on a platter with other antipasti.

Serves 4.

CROCHETTE DI PATATE AL FORMAGGIO
POTATO-CHEESE CROQUETTES

2 pounds potatoes, peeled and cut into chunks
4 tablespoons butter
4 eggs
1/2 cup grated Romano cheese
1/4 cup chopped fresh parsley
1 1/2 teaspoons salt
1/2 teaspoon pepper
1/2 cup Italian bread crumbs, seasoned
2 cups light olive oil

Even though most Americans associate Parmesan cheese with Italian cooking, my family has always used Romano. Get the best quality you can find, grate it fresh—and you'll see why! But, if Parmesan really is your favorite, you can use it instead of the Romano in this recipe.

Boil the potatoes until they are tender, then drain and transfer to a large mixing bowl. Mash the potatoes and beat in the butter, 2 eggs, the cheese, parsley, salt, and pepper. Cover, and chill for at least an hour in the refrigerator.

In a small mixing bowl, whip the other 2 eggs. Form the potato mixture into small walnut-size balls. Dip and coat the croquettes in the egg, then in the bread crumbs. Heat the olive oil in a medium skillet over low to medium heat. Fry the croquettes in the oil until they are golden brown. Serve immediately.

Makes 2 dozen.

PIUMINI DI MOZZARELLA AL FORNO
MOZZARELLA CHEESE PUFFS

2 cups flour
1/2 teaspoon salt
1/2 teaspoon paprika
1 cup butter
1 pound shredded Mozzarella cheese

My family has always used fresh Mozzarella in our antipasi. I will always remember the wonderful fragrance of fresh Mozzarella every time I entered my parents' deli. They made it in the back room on a big coal stove, and if you have never experienced fresh, homemade Mozzarella, travel to the ends of the earth to find it, believe me! This dish will help you understand why Italians have such a great love for this cheese.

Preheat the oven to 350°F.

Sift the dry ingredients together. In a large mixing bowl, cream the butter, then mix in the Mozzarella cheese. Add the flour mixture and mix well.

Shape into small balls and place on an ungreased baking sheet. Bake for 15 to 20 minutes, or until the balls are puffed and golden brown. *Makes 1 dozen.*

MINESTRA E ZUPPE
SOUPS & STEWS

What comes to mind when you think "soup" and "Italian"? *Minestrone*. And it's no wonder. If you look at the menus of most Italian restaurants in America, that's the soup you see.

When we were working on this book, my son Neil learned the history of that Italian classic, minestrone: in the early days, Italy was comprised of many small kingdoms, and they were always at war with each other. Because of this, travel was risky. Peasants barred their doors at dark in fear of unfriendly soldiers. Inns were few and far between. So travelers depended on monasteries for sustenance. Each morning the monks prepared thick meat and vegetable soup from whatever was fresh from the monastery garden, feeding it to hungry travelers each evening, never refusing anyone their hospitality. The word *minestrone* even comes from a Latin word that means "to hand over."

I like the spirit behind that story. It is the same when I cook for my family—I can never refuse them. Like I told my granddaughter the other day, "When you cook for your family, think about each one of them, and then cook for them, loving each one the whole time."

Italian cooks have mastered the art of making every kind of soup. So when you say you want to cook everything from soup to nuts, don't just stop there. Tell me what kind of soup! Do you want fish soup, meat soup, or vegetable soup? Do you want the broth thick or thin? How about a cream soup? Italians make them all.

Look in this section, and you will see what I mean: there are soups with herbs, with seafood, with beans, with meat, with pasta, rice, or polenta. There are soups with tomatoes, onions, celery, carrots, string beans, peas, spinach, escarole, zucchini, potatoes, cabbage, leeks, and red and green peppers. There are recipes for vegetable soups that have been passed down in my family for generations from mother to daughter, and a recipe for *cacciucco* (fish soup), which has been made in southern Italy for more than three thousand years. Even minestrone itself is a fifteen-hundred-year-old soup.

Soups, like sauces, often become even more delicious a day or two after they are made. So you might want to make your soups in extra large quantities—you can even freeze them for "instant" soup to serve a surprise guest or at a spontaneous family get-together later on. But whatever you do, never freeze a soup containing pasta. Freezing makes pasta turn mushy, and mushy pasta is a sin.

PASTA & WHITE BEAN SOUP

½ pound cannellini (white
   kidney) beans
½ pound ceci (garbanzo) beans
¼ cup olive oil
2 tablespoons minced garlic
l large onion, chopped
2 stalks celery, chopped
1 pound ripe tomatoes, chopped
4 cups chicken or vegetable broth
½ teaspoon oregano
2 large bay leaves
1 teaspoon salt
½ teaspoon pepper
½ pound spaghetti
   (broken into 1-inch pieces)

This recipe came from Foggia, Italy, where Mammanon came from. It's the Neapolitan way of cooking the dish. My son-in-law Joey, who is Sicilian and a terrific cook, makes his version much thicker, and with about twice as much olive oil. Both ways are good. To save time, you can make it with canned beans, but it has much more flavor when you use the dried beans.

In a large pot, combine the two types of beans, cover with a couple of inches of water, and soak overnight.

The next day, drain the beans, cover them in fresh water, and bring to a boil.

Lower the heat and let simmer for 1 hour (you may have to add additional water).

Add the olive oil, garlic, onions, celery, tomatoes and their juice, another 2 cups of water, and the broth. Bring again to a boil. Add the oregano, bay leaves, salt, and pepper. Turn down the heat and let simmer for 1 hour.

Fill another large pot with water and bring to a boil. Add a teaspoon of olive oil and the spaghetti pieces. Cook the spaghetti al dente, drain, and add to the simmering soup just a few minutes before you are ready to serve. Serve in soup bowls with a nice loaf of Italian bread, and always put some crushed hot red peppers on the table (some people like this soup with a little zest).

Serves 4.

VARIATION

You can put meat in this dish, and sometimes, particularly on a cold day, I will add Italian sausage for the kids. Simply cut 1 or 2 pounds of the sausage into small pieces. Rinse a skillet and leave in the moisture. Sauté the sausage pieces until lightly browned and add to the soup when it is about half-way done. The sausage will give the soup a nice, rich flavor.

This is my wedding day. From left to right: my brother Jimmy, Mammanon, me, my husband Gaetano, my brother Tony, and Poppanon.

PASTA & LENTIL SOUP

1 pound lentils

2 tablespoons olive oil

3 large stalks celery, diced

2 large carrots, diced

1 large onion, diced

1 pound pancetta (bacon) or
ham, chopped

1 tablespoon minced garlic

1 tablespoon sweet basil

1 teaspoon sage

2 bay leaves

6 cups chicken broth

2 cups precooked pasta (small
pieces of spaghetti or pastini)

Salt and pepper to taste

½ cup freshly grated Romano
cheese

Whenever Mammanon used dried beans in a dish, she always cooked them with a few bay leaves. She said that bay leaves are "good for the stomach." In other words, they're good for digestion. When my children were babies, I would boil bay leaves in water and give them this herbal water in their bottles. It settled their tummies every time.

Cover the lentils with a few inches of water and soak overnight, discarding any that float to the top. The following day, rinse the lentils and put them in a large pot, covering them again with 2 to 3 inches of water. Bring to a boil, then cover and reduce the heat. Simmer for 1 hour.

Add the olive oil, celery, carrots, onion, pancetta or ham, garlic, basil, sage, and bay leaves. Simmer for 45 minutes, adding more water if you need to.

When the lentils are soft and the soup is thick, stir in the chicken broth. Continue to simmer for another 30 minutes or so, adding more water or broth to achieve the consistency you prefer.

When the soup is the proper consistency, add the pasta and season with salt and pepper to taste. Serve in soup bowls with the grated cheese on the side.

Serves 4.

Z U P P A   D I   M E R L U Z Z O
WHITING SOUP

4 cups chicken or vegetable broth
2 cups water
¼ cup olive oil
2 large carrots, diced
1 large onion, diced
3 large stalks celery, diced
1 heaping tablespoon minced
  garlic
1 pound plum tomatoes
  (fresh or canned), chopped
2 tablespoons pimentos, chopped
½ cup chopped fresh parsley
1 tablespoon chopped fresh basil
1 tablespoon chopped fresh
  oregano
1 cup dry white wine
2 pounds whiting fish fillet
Salt and pepper to taste

Whiting is primarily an east coast fish. If you are unable to get it, you can substitute any light-colored fish. Ling cod is an excellent alternative.

Fill a large pot with the broth and water, and bring to a boil.

Heat the olive oil in a large skillet, add the diced vegetables, and sauté over medium heat until tender. Add the garlic and chopped tomatoes with their juice, and simmer for about 5 minutes. Add the sautéed mixture to the pot, along with the pimentos, parsley, basil, oregano, and wine. It is always best to use these herbs fresh if possible. They

lend a much more pure and aromatic flavor to any dish. However, if the fresh herbs aren't available to you, substitute dried herbs.

Boil the soup for 10 minutes. Put the whiting into the boiling mixture, cover, and turn the heat down low. Simmer for 30 minutes. (Whiting falls apart in the soup into small chunks and is very tender.)

Season with salt and pepper and serve hot.
Serves 4.

CHICKEN & VEGETABLE STEW

1 stewing chicken (3 to 4 pounds),
  cut into 8 pieces
1 large onion, diced
1/8 cup minced garlic
2 large carrots, diced
2 large stalks celery, diced
1/2 pound string beans,
  cut into 1/2-inch pieces
1 pound fresh plum tomatoes, diced
1 teaspoon oregano
3 bay leaves
Salt and pepper to taste
1 1/2 cups frozen peas
1 cup grated Romano cheese

Mammanon often made her chicken stew for her Sunday dinners. Then with the leftover stew the next day, she would add a little of this, a little of that—to make the family think they were getting a brand new soup. She tricked us every time!

Rinse a large pot, and leave the moisture in it. Brown the chicken pieces over medium heat (this brings out the chicken's natural oils). Add the onions and garlic, and sauté them with the chicken until the onions are clear.

Fill the pot one-half full with water. Add the sautéed chicken mixture, carrots, celery, and string beans. Bring to a boil. Add the tomatoes,

oregano, bay leaves, salt, and pepper. Turn down the heat and simmer for 1 hour.

Remove the stew from the heat, transfer the chicken pieces to a cutting board, and remove all the bones. Shred the chicken and then return the shredded chicken to the pot. Add the frozen peas and bring the pot to a simmer. Simmer for 10 minutes and serve immediately. I like to serve the stew with a bowl of grated cheese on the table. Some of my family like this stew with crushed chili peppers. *Serves 4 to 6.*

PASTA & FAVA BEAN SOUP

1 pound fava (lima) beans
1/4 cup olive oil
1 tablespoon minced garlic
2 large carrots, diced
1 large onion, diced
2 large stalks celery, diced
1 pound ripe plum tomatoes, diced
4 cups chicken broth
1/2 cup chopped fresh parsley
1 teaspoon oregano
2 bay leaves
Salt and pepper to taste
1 pound small pasta (egg noodles,
  macaroni), cooked

With most of my bean and vegetable soups, I prefer to cook the beans quite well, until they are very soft and dissolve into the soup. However, because fava beans have such a unique and delicious flavor, I cook them a little less so that they stay somewhat firm in this soup. And don't forget the bay leaves in any bean dish— they really help your digestion!

Soak the beans overnight. The next day, drain them, place them in a large pot, and cover with a few inches of fresh water. Bring to a boil, then turn down the heat and let simmer.

Meanwhile, put the olive oil in a large skillet and add the garlic, carrots, onion, and celery.

Sauté for a few minutes. Add the tomatoes. Simmer this for 5 minutes, then remove from the heat. When the fava beans are beginning to get tender, add the vegetable mixture to the soup. Add the chicken broth and bring to a boil. Add the parsley, oregano, and bay leaves. Turn down the heat and simmer for another 30 minutes or so—until the beans are quite tender but still hold together. Season with salt and pepper.

Right before serving the soup, add the pre-cooked pasta to the pot and stir. Do not let the pasta cook in the soup. Serve hot in soup bowls with a pinch of chopped fresh parsley. *Serves 4.*

EGG RIBBON SOUP

8 cups clear chicken broth
1 cup chopped spinach (optional)
3 large eggs, beaten
1/2 cup chopped fresh parsley
Salt and pepper to taste
1 cup grated Romano cheese

This is the fastest soup to make, and so satisfying on a cold evening. The quickest way of making it is to use canned chicken stock. And to tell the truth, these days I do that sometimes. But the way I learned (and, of course, you should do it this way if you want the freshest soup) was to make a fresh chicken soup, but to strain out the vegetables and chicken and just use the stock. I sometimes will make a big pot of this and freeze it for use in future soups.

In a large pot, bring the broth to a simmer. Do not boil. While the soup is simmering, slowly pour the eggs into the soup, then remove the pan from the heat. The eggs will immediately cook. If you want spinach in your soup (fresh or frozen spinach will do), add it to the chicken broth before you add the eggs, and simmer for 10 minutes. Stir in the parsley and season with salt and pepper. Serve in soup bowls with some grated cheese on top. *Serves 4.*

ESCAROLE SOUP

1 chicken, cut into 8 pieces, or
    4 to 6 breasts
2 large carrots, diced
2 large stalks celery, diced
1 large onion, diced
1 large bunch escarole, shredded
1/2 cup chopped fresh parsley
Salt and pepper to taste

Escarole soup is one of my favorites, and I make it often. Before you add the escarole to the soup, you can always steam the escarole first, keeping the escarole water to drink, and adding the escarole to the soup. My mother always did this. She said it was good for the stomach. In fact, as children, if we had any kind of a stomachache, she would always give us either escarole broth or bay leaf broth as a remedy.

Place the chicken and 6 to 8 cups of water in a large pot and bring it to a boil. If your chicken comes with giblets, chop the liver and add it to the soup for a richer stock. Do not remove the skin from the chicken, at least not all of it, because this helps to create a richer soup as well. Add the carrots, celery, and onion. Turn down the heat, cover, and simmer for an hour.

Remove the chicken to shred it (discard the bones), and then return the chicken to the soup. Add the escarole and parsley, cover, and simmer for 15 minutes. Season with salt and pepper.

Serves 4 to 6.

VARIATIONS

1. For Easter, my mother used to make escarole soup with breast of lamb instead of chicken. She'd cook the lamb in the chicken broth and vegetables, then shred the lamb and put it in the soup with the escarole. This was traditional for our Easter dinner.

2. ESCAROLE SOUP WITH MEATBALLS: Prepare the recipe above but do not return the chicken to the soup (or start out with canned chicken broth instead). Prepare the Meatballs (see page 102), but make them very, very small so they won't fall apart. Brown them lightly, then add them to the soup. This makes a delicious, rich soup.

3. At the last minute, you might add some beaten eggs, as you do in the Stracciatella Soup (see page 33).

4. You can also add precooked noodles to this soup if you like. Try small egg noodles, pastini, or any small-size pasta.

That's my uncle Angelo, when he had just come to the U.S. from Italy.

MINESTRONE SOUP

1 cup diced onion
$\frac{1}{8}$ cup minced garlic
$\frac{1}{4}$ cup olive oil
1 cup chopped cabbage
1 cup green beans in $\frac{1}{2}$-inch pieces
1 cup diced zucchini squash
3 large potatoes, peeled and diced
3 stalks celery, diced
3 carrots, diced
3 cups chopped tomatoes with
   their juice
8 cups chicken stock
2 cups water
1 tablespoon sage
1 tablespoon fresh basil
$\frac{1}{4}$ cup fresh parsley

1 cup precooked red kidney beans
$\frac{1}{2}$ pound spaghetti, broken
   into 1-inch pieces
$\frac{1}{2}$ pound pancetta (optional)
Salt and pepper to taste

I like to make many of my soups with a lot of fresh parsley, but when my children were small they didn't like the parsley. So to still give the soup a parsley taste, I would tie a large bunch of fresh parsley to a string, cook it in the soup, then before serving take it out. You can do this with other herbs as well. This method gives any soup or sauce a subtle and delicious flavor.

Sauté the onion and garlic in the olive oil until the onion is tender. Add the chopped vegetables and tomatoes, and simmer for 10 minutes.

Transfer to a large pot, add the chicken stock and water, and bring to a boil. If you choose to add the bacon, slice it into small strips and add to the soup. Add the herbs, turn down the heat, and simmer for 1/2 hour. Add the kidney beans and broken spaghetti pieces, and cook until the spaghetti is tender, about 10 minutes. Season with salt and pepper.

Serves 4 to 6.

WHITE BEAN SOUP

1 $\frac{1}{2}$ pounds dried cannellini beans,
   cooked and drained
6 cups chicken broth
1 large red bell pepper, minced
1 large green bell pepper, minced
1 large onion, minced
1 tablespoon minced garlic
$\frac{1}{4}$ cup olive oil
1 tablespoon sweet basil
Salt and pepper to taste

I often make this soup around the holidays. As you will see, the colors are perfect for a festive look. Instead of cooking the peppers in the soup you can steam them until they are tender. Blend the red pepper into a purée, then the green. After the soup is seasoned to taste, swirl a small amount of the green and red purée around in each bowl of bean soup, making an elegant red and green design. This is sure to impress your family and friends.

Purée the beans with the chicken broth, and simmer in a large pot over very low heat.

In a medium-size skillet, sauté the red and green peppers, onion, and garlic in the olive oil until the peppers are tender. Stir this into the puréed beans, along with the basil. Salt and pepper to taste, then simmer for 5 to 10 minutes and serve. Garnish each bowl with a sprig of fresh basil.

For a spicy version of this soup, sauté a few minced green chili peppers with the onions and add to the soup. Be sure to wear rubber gloves when chopping these peppers, or their zing will go right into your fingers!

Serves 4 to 6.

SPINACH POLENTA SOUP

1 pound spinach
8 cups chicken or vegetable broth
2 tablespoons butter
1 tablespoon flour
2 cups half & half
4 tablespoons polenta meal
2 tablespoons minced garlic
1 teaspoon nutmeg
Salt and pepper to taste

This is a very old recipe, going back a long time in my family. It is very soothing to the tummy, and it makes you feel warm inside. Maybe that's why it was always such a favorite with my kids when they were young.

In a covered pot, simmer the spinach in the chicken broth until the spinach is well cooked. In a blender or food processor, purée the spinach and broth until it's smooth and then return it to the pot.

Melt the butter in a small saucepan. Stir in the flour, making a paste. Gradually stir in the half & half. Stir in the polenta meal. Cook this over low heat, stirring continuously, until it thickens. Stir in the garlic and the nutmeg, and then add this to the blended spinach mixture, stirring continuously. Cover and simmer over low heat for another 15 minutes, stirring frequently. Season with salt and pepper and serve immediately.

Serves 4 to 6.

In the old days, Poppanon used to make wine in the basement below the deli that he and Mammanon ran. Every wine season, it was a ritual: In October, the flatbed truck would pull up in front of almost every house on our street. I remember seeing the big boxes of red grapes stacked up on the sidewalk all the way down the street. And I remember my son helping his father and his grandfather carry the boxes of grapes down into the cellar, just like the boys next door would be helping their fathers and their grandfathers, and so on down the street. The next day, you could smell the grapes being crushed and the wine being made all through the neighborhood.

One year, when my son Neil was only five, Poppanon taught him about wine making in the Old Country. I'll let him tell the story:

"In the basement of the deli, Poppanon had a huge barrel-like tub that he used to make his wine in. One year, I was alone down there with him as he started to press the grapes in the wine vat. I was very excited about the wine making that was happening all over the neighborhood, and I asked Poppanon how they made wine in Italy. He told me that they didn't use a press like the one he was using. 'No,' he said, almost all in Italian, 'when I was growing up, the kids would get in the wine vat and we would squish the grapes with our feet.'

I immediately tried to climb in the wine vat; I couldn't wait to try it. 'No, no, no,' he laughed. 'You have to take off your shoes and socks and roll up your pants!' So I did, and I climbed right in, jumping up and down on the grapes as hard as I could.

My father heard the rucus first, and he came down to see what was happening. When he saw me jumping around in the wine vat, he started laughing and teasing Poppanon that he was going to get me drunk on the aroma, the musty, thick smell of the crushed grapes. Soon Mammanon and Elodia heard the commotion, and they came running down too, giggling away at my enthusiam for the old style of making wine."

FISH SOUP

1 large onion, diced
3 stalks celery, diced
¼ cup olive oil
¼ cup butter
2 cups chopped tomatoes
1 tablespoon minced garlic
8 cups chicken broth
2 cups water
1 cup dry white wine
⅛ teaspoon saffron
¼ cup chopped fresh parsley
Salt and pepper to taste
2 pounds merluzzo (whiting)
1 dozen mussels
1 dozen clams

Merluzzo (whiting) is primarily an east coast fish. In other areas of the country, you may substitute any fresh white fish or even red snapper. For something a little more special I will often add fresh lobster meat as well, and even a few shrimp. Be sure to serve this soup with warm, fresh, crusty Italian bread. You will surely want to dip pieces of it in the delicious broth.

In a large pot, sauté the onion and celery over low heat in the olive oil and butter for a few minutes. Add the tomatoes with their juices, along with the garlic. Let this simmer for 10 minutes. Add the chicken broth, water, and wine, and bring to a boil. Add the saffron and chopped parsley, and season with salt and pepper. Simmer this broth for another 15 minutes. Chop the fish into small chunks and add to the soup.

In another pan, steam the clams and mussels over medium heat until they open. Add these, along with the water used to steam them, to the soup and simmer another 10 minutes.

Serves 4 to 6.

There's Gaetano, my husband, in the middle of all my girl-friends! (That's me next to him on the left.) We're at Coney Island in the 1940s. I always packed a big picnic lunch so we could talk, and swim, and sunbathe all day long.

ZUPPA D'ARAGOSTA
LOBSTER SOUP

6 cups chicken broth

2 cups water

2 pounds lobster meat

¼ cup + 1 tablespoon olive oil

3 stalks celery, diced

1 large onion, diced

1 tablespoon minced garlic

4 cups chopped tomatoes
  with their juice

1 cup dry white wine

1 tablespoon basil

¼ cup butter

¼ cup flour

3 cups milk (half & half for a
  creamier soup)

Salt and pepper to taste

This soup is a very special, elegant soup. It is somewhat more expensive to make, so you might want to save it for your special guests or your most important occasions.

In a large pot, bring the chicken broth and water to a boil. Chop up the lobster meat into small pieces and add it to the boiling liquid. Cover, turn down the heat, and let simmer.

In a skillet, heat a tablespoon of the olive oil and add the celery, onion, and garlic. Sauté over medium heat, taking care not to brown. Add the tomatoes, wine, and the basil, and sauté for another 5 to 10 minutes. Add this to the lobster mixture and continue to simmer the soup for 30 minutes, covered, over very low heat.

In a medium saucepan, melt the butter and mix in the remaining olive oil, then the flour. Whisk in the milk gradually, stirring continuously. When it begins to thicken (just when it begins, not when it gets real thick!), stir this mixture gradually into the simmering soup. Be sure the soup does not boil after this point but is stirred and simmered over very low heat.

Remove half of the soup and blend it in a high-speed blender until smooth. Half of the soup should retain flakes of the tender lobster meat and chopped vegetables. Mix in the blended soup with the lobster mixture. Season with salt and pepper.

Serve this soup with fresh Italian bread or maybe topped with some Italian-bread croutons. *Serves 4 to 6.*

ZUPPA DI COZZE
MUSSEL SOUP

1 large onion
1 tablespoon minced garlic
2 tablespoons olive oil
8 cups vegetable broth
1/2 cup minced parsley
1 tablespoon sweet basil
2 pints mussels, shelled
1 cup grated carrots
1/4 cup butter
2 tablespoons all-purpose flour
1 cup white wine
1 cup half & half
Salt and pepper to taste

This soup can also be a delicious sauce for pasta. Make it a little thicker than you would for a soup, and use it on top of linguini or fettuccine.

Slice the onion in half, then in thin arcs. Sauté with the garlic in the olive oil until the onion is clear (be sure not to brown).

Bring the vegetable broth to a boil in a large pot. Add the sautéed onion mixture, the parsley and basil, and then the mussels. Reduce the heat, cover, and simmer for 20 minutes. Stir in the carrots.

In a small saucepan, melt the butter and stir in the flour. Immediately whisk in the wine and half & half. Stir constantly until the mixture begins to thicken. Stir the mixture gradually into the soup, being careful not to bring the soup to a boil. Keep it on a very low simmer. Season with salt and pepper and serve garnished with some extra grated carrot.

Serves 4.

PUMPKIN SOUP

6 cups precooked pumpkin
6 cups milk
1/4 cup minced fresh parsley
1 tablespoon brown sugar
3 tablespoons butter
Salt and pepper to taste
Herbed croutons

This is a delicious soup any time of year, but for a treat, try chilling it in the summer months and serving it along with a chilled white wine.

Using a whisk, combine the pumpkin with the milk in a large saucepan. (For a creamier version, substitute half & half for part of the milk.) Stir in the parsley and sugar. Add the butter, cover, and simmer for about 15 minutes, stirring regularly so that the soup doesn't stick to the bottom of the pan. Season with salt and pepper. If you prefer a thicker soup, stir in more pumpkin. Serve hot, garnished with croutons.   *Serves 4.*

CHESTNUT SOUP

1 pound chestnuts
8 cups vegetable broth
2 tablespoons olive oil
1 cup chopped onion
1 cup chopped celery
2 carrots, grated
2 cups milk
Salt and pepper to taste
1/4 cup minced fresh parsley
   (for garnish)

Chestnuts are a food I always associate with the Old Country—to me, they have a very traditional, Old World taste. Mammanon used chestnuts in her cooking quite a bit, a custom she brought with her from Italy. I always use fresh chestnuts when I make this soup, but since cooking with chestnuts is not as common in America, you might not always be able to find them fresh in your local market. You can make a very good version of this soup using canned chestnuts.

If you choose to use fresh chestnuts, score them across the rounded side with a sharp knife and bake them in a 350°F oven for 15 to 20 minutes, or until tender. While they are still warm, peel off their shells and skins. In a large pot, heat up the vegetable broth and then blend it with the peeled chestnuts in a high-speed blender until smooth. Transfer back to the pot and simmer over very low heat.

In a medium-size skillet, heat the olive oil and add the onions and celery. Sauté over low heat until the vegetables are tender. Add this to the chestnut mixture. Stir in the grated carrots, along with the milk, and simmer for 15 minutes. Be sure not to boil. Season with salt and pepper and serve garnished with a sprinkling of fresh parsley.
Serves 4 to 6.

CREAM OF ASPARAGUS SOUP

2 pounds fresh asparagus
3 cups diced potatoes
1 cup diced leeks
1/2 cup chopped onion
2 quarts chicken or vegetable broth
2 egg yolks
1 cup cream or half & half
Salt and pepper to taste

This is a classic soup—and one of my son's favorites. If you use vegetable broth instead of chicken broth, you can serve it to your vegetarian friends.

Wash the asparagus, cutting away and discarding the tough ends. Cut off a dozen or so of the tips (about 1 inch down) and set aside. Chop the rest of the asparagus.

In a large pot, combine the chopped asparagus, potatoes, leeks, onion, and broth. Bring to a boil, then turn down the heat, cover, and simmer for 30 minutes. Remove the pan from the heat and blend the soup to a smooth consistency in a blender or food processor. Return the soup to the pot, add most of the reserved asparagus tips (putting a few aside for garnish later), and continue to simmer.

In a small mixing bowl, beat the egg yolks and cream together. Remove the soup from the heat and whisk in the egg yolk and cream mixture, whisking continuously to prevent curdling. Add salt and pepper, and serve each bowl of soup topped with a few asparagus tips, accompanied by some fresh, warm, and crusty Italian bread.   *Serves 6.*

PASTASCIUTTA E RISO
PASTA & RICE

People seem to think Italian food means pasta, pasta, and more pasta. But if that were true, there wouldn't be nine sections in this book! No, the cooking Mammanon learned in Apulia, Italy, contains a broad range of dishes, and so does the cooking of other Italian immigrant families I have known in America.

On the other hand, for my family and for all Italian families, pasta is the soul of the cuisine: You eat a nice plate of pasta with a good sauce and you feel good. As I have told my children many times, pasta is the best food to make you feel loved. Pasta *is* love! That is why this section on pasta and rice is so large.

Why pasta and rice? There is a history to why pasta and rice are both so important in my family's diet. That history has to do with the geography of Italy. Approximately 220 miles south of Rome, there is a natural frontier formed by mountains and rivers that cuts across the Italian countryside. There is an ancient road built along this frontier, a road built by the Romans. It was named Via Saleria, the Salt Way, because it ended at the salt marshes of the Adriatic Sea. I have been told that Via Saleria was the first great trade route of the Roman Empire—and they built it so well that it is still used today.

Via Saleria divides Poppanon and Mammanon's homeland into "northern Italy" and "southern Italy." Before Italy became unified, the north was the land of rice (risotto) and polenta (although not quite as much). The south was pasta country. When Italy became one country, the south learned about risotto from the north, and the north learned about pasta from the south. Today, every region has both risotto and pasta dishes. That is why the cooking that Mammanon learned in Apulia, which was located in "southern Italy," contains both. And that is why you will find both in the cooking of all Italian Americans.

Risotto and pasta both have a somewhat neutral taste. You might even call them bland. That is why the sauce and other ingredients you use define the dish. However, cooking a pasta dish is very different from cooking a risotto dish. With pasta, you add the sauce after you boil the pasta. With risotto, you add most of the flavoring from the start. Cooking rice slowly with the herbs, spices, meat, or fish in the same liquid as the rice—each grain absorbing flavor as it swells—is fundamental to good risotto preparation.

There is another big difference between risotto and pasta, and that is shape. Because risotto is a whole grain, it comes in one basic shape and that is it. Pasta, though, is made from flour—and you can make it into almost any shape you want! There are more than fifty different shapes of pasta in every region of Italy. In Apulia, some of the most popular pasta shapes are orecchiette, shaped like little ears; conchiglie, shaped like seashells; and fusilli, twisted strands.

Apart from the shape, there are two other forms that pasta comes in: dried pasta made in factories, and fresh pasta made at home or in small local specialty shops. When my kids were growing up, I made most of our pasta myself. Now that I am older, I use the dried pasta more often than I used to, but I still try to find fresh pasta whenever I can because fresh is so much better.

The other day, my son Neil was talking about pasta-making in our family that he remembers: "Countless times, I've seen Mammanon and Elodia make dozens of different kinds of pasta from scratch and by hand—without pasta machines. (And the way they did it—with no water, and only eggs to moisten the flour—made the lightest, most delicate pasta imaginable.) When I was little, and they had me in the kitchen with them, I had my own little pile of pasta dough that Mammanon or Elodia had prepared. I can remember working real hard to cut the dough into the shape of fettuccine, or whatever type of pasta they were making, but it took me a long time to get even a little pile of pasta in the shape I wanted. Then I'd look over at them, my mother and my grandmother chattering away, their fingers flying, and they'd have these enormous stacks of shaped pasta. They must have been a hundred times faster than me."

Whether you use fresh or dried, you will be amazed—I still am—at how each pasta shape changes the flavor of every pasta dish, even when the same sauce is used. Every kind of pasta holds the sauce a little differently. With so many shapes of pasta to choose from, and such a wide variety of sauces and ways to prepare it, who could ever get tired of pasta!

SPAGHETTI WITH GARLIC & OIL

1 pound spaghetti

$^1/_2$ cup olive oil

$^1/_4$ cup minced garlic

1 tablespoon chopped fresh basil

$^1/_2$ cup chopped fresh parsley

$^3/_4$ cup grated Romano cheese

1 cup Italian bread crumbs, seasoned
   (optional)

1 teaspoon crushed chili peppers
   (optional)

Salt and pepper to taste

This dish is so simple to make, yet it is so tasty! And it really is many dishes in one, because if you add any one of the optional ingredients, you have a completely different dish. Mammanon always prepared it piping hot, but I tried adding some fresh vegetables, refrigerating it and serving it as a chilled pasta salad in the summer months—and it was terrific. Try it that way too.

Bring a large pot of water to a boil. Add the spaghetti and cook al dente. Rinse and drain.

In a skillet, heat the oil and lightly sauté the garlic until golden. Place the pasta in a large pasta bowl and add the garlic oil and herbs. Be sure all of the spaghetti is well coated.

Depending on your tastes, you may want to sprinkle in some extra olive oil at this point, or perhaps, for garlic lovers, more minced garlic. Toss the pasta with the freshly grated cheese and if you choose, add any of the optional ingredients. Season with salt and pepper, and serve immediately.   *Serves 4.*

NOTE: This recipe works well with linguini, spaghettini, or just about any type of pasta.

LASAGNA

$^1/_2$ recipe Brooklyn Meat "Gravy"
   (see page 158)

1 teaspoon olive oil

1 $^1/_2$ pounds lasagna noodles
   (boxed or fresh)

1 pound Ricotta cheese

2 large eggs

2 cups grated Romano cheese

1 $^1/_2$ pounds shredded Mozzarella
   cheese

$^1/_2$ cup minced parsley

1 teaspoon salt

$^1/_2$ teaspoon pepper

My family told me that I shouldn't include our recipe for lasagna in my book because "everybody knows how to make lasagna." Well, perhaps that's true, but my mother taught me to make it this way, I taught it to my daughters and granddaughters, and it didn't seem right not to include it—so enjoy!

Remove the sausages and meatballs from the Brooklyn Meat "Gravy," chop, and set aside.

Bring a large pot of salted water to a boil. Add the olive oil and the pasta, and cook the noodles al dente. Rinse and drain the noodles, then lay them out flat and set aside.

Preheat the oven to 350°F. In a medium-size mixing bowl, beat the Ricotta cheese and eggs until smooth and creamy. Reserve a few handfuls of shredded Mozzarella to sprinkle on top of the dish before it goes into the oven. Add the Romano, the rest of the shredded Mozzarella, the parsley, salt, and pepper to the Ricotta mixture. Mix well.

Spread a thin layer of the Meat "Gravy" on the bottom of a large baking dish. Reserve some sauce for serving with your lasagna later. Cover with a layer of the lasagna noodles. Spread a layer of the Ricotta cheese mixture smoothly on top. Cover with a layer of chopped meats and another layer of pasta. Spread some more sauce, and continue layering in this manner until the baking dish is full. Top off the dish with a thin layer of sauce and shredded Mozzarella cheese.

Bake for 30 minutes. Be sure not to brown the top layer of cheese. Remove the pan from the oven and set aside for 10 minutes to settle before cutting into pieces. I like to spoon some of the reserved meat sauce onto the individual serving plates and put a slice of the lasagna down in the middle of it.
                              Serves 6 to 8.

V A R I A T I O N S

1. For a meatless alternative, try substituting the Marinara Sauce (see page 164) for the Meat "Gravy," omitting the chopped sausages and meatballs, and adding a layer of sautéed vegetables such as onions and spinach.

2. Instead of using lasagna noodles, you can substitute any type of pasta noodle as long as it's a fairly large noodle (rigatoni, fusilli, or ziti). Baked ziti is one of my children's favorite pasta dishes to this day. As in other recipes in this book, each type of pasta makes a unique dish.

PASTA WITH PEAS

2 tablespoons + 1 teaspoon
  olive oil

1 medium-size onion, chopped

1 tablespoon minced garlic

4 to 5 soft, ripe plum tomatoes,
  diced

1 pound green peas

1 cup chicken broth

1 teaspoon basil

Salt and pepper to taste

1/2 teaspoon sugar

1/2 pound bacon

1 pound bucatini pasta

1 cup grated Romano cheese

I usually make this dish using bucatini pasta, which is a small, round pasta with a hole in the center. Even though this is our family favorite with this dish, the recipe works well with almost any type of pasta.

In a large skillet, combine 2 tablespoons of the olive oil with the onion and garlic, and sauté over medium heat, being careful not to brown. Add the tomatoes, peas, chicken broth, basil, salt, pepper, and sugar. Cover, and simmer over low heat for about 20 minutes.

Brown the bacon in another skillet. Drain off the fat, then break into pieces and add to the simmering mixture.

Bring a large pot of salted water to a boil. Add the remaining teaspoon of olive oil and the pasta, and cook al dente. Drain and toss with the grated cheese. Stir in the pea mixture and serve.

Serves 4 to 6.

PASTA WITH PROSCIUTTO & ARTICHOKES

1 pound tagliatelle pasta

1 onion, diced

2 tablespoons butter

2 tablespoons olive oil

1 cup chopped artichoke hearts

Juice of 1 lemon

1/2 pound prosciutto, julienned

2 cups chopped tomatoes

1/4 cup chopped fresh parsley

1/2 cup white wine

1 cup half & half

Salt and pepper to taste

1 cup grated Romano cheese

Prosciutto is a rich and delicious type of Italian ham, and we use it in a wide variety of antipasti, pastas, main courses, and, of course, sandwiches. It is sliced paper-thin, so its wonderful flavors easily blend into any dish you use it in.

Bring a large pot of salted water to a boil, add the pasta, and cook al dente. Rinse the pasta, drain, and set aside.

Preheat the oven to 375°F.

In a large skillet, sauté the onion in the butter and olive oil. Add the artichoke hearts, lemon juice, prosciutto, tomatoes, parsley, and wine. Cover and simmer for 20 minutes. Stir in the half & half. Remove from the heat and season with salt and pepper.

Transfer the pasta to a large mixing bowl and stir in the sauce. Blend all the ingredients well with the pasta and transfer to a large baking dish. Cover the pasta with the grated Romano, and bake for 10 minutes. *Serves 4 to 6.*

My son Neil, my daughter Annette, and, in the middle, my daughter Marilyn. Marilyn was known as "baby doll" because she was so pretty.

MRS. BICE'S RAVIOLI

6 cups flour

$^1/_2$ cup olive oil

2 large eggs

1 $^1/_2$ tablespoons salt

1 $^1/_2$ cups warm water

2 bunches swiss chard

1 loaf Italian bread

2 cups milk

1 large onion, chopped

2 cups chopped mushrooms

$^1/_2$ cup chopped fresh parsley

1 tablespoon minced garlic

1 tablespoon butter

2 tablespoons olive oil

1 teaspoon rosemary

1 teaspoon marjoram

1 pound ground veal

1 pound ground beef

6 eggs, whipped

1 teaspoon salt

$^1/_2$ teaspoon pepper

$^3/_4$ cup grated Romano cheese

1 recipe Marinara Sauce
   (see page 164)

Mrs. Bice was my mother's friend. Whenever she came to my mother's apartment for dinner, she always brought her delicious ravioli. She never would give me the recipe, but I finally convinced her to let me watch her make them. They take a little time to do, so I only make them for special occasions. But then I freeze a big container of them for the next time.

Combine the flour, olive oil, 2 eggs, salt, and water in a large mixing bowl and stir until a stiff ball is formed. Turn onto a floured baking board and knead until pliable (approximately 5 minutes). Cover the dough with a cloth and let sit for 1 hour.

Steam the swiss chard and drain on paper towels until all the excess water is out. Chop finely and set aside. Remove the crust from the Italian bread, and soak both in milk until softened. Squeeze out the excess milk, and set aside.

In a large skillet, sauté the onion, mushrooms, parsley, and garlic in the butter and olive oil. Add the swiss chard, rosemary, and marjoram, and continue sautéing until all the moisture has evaporated. Set aside to cool.

In another skillet, sauté the ground meats in a small amount of olive oil and set aside. In a large mixing bowl, combine the eggs, Italian bread, sautéed vegetables, sautéed meat, salt, pepper, and grated cheese.

Roll the dough out as thinly as possible into a rectangle shape. Spread the filling evenly over one half of the dough and fold the other half of the dough over the top to cover the filling. Using a ravioli pin, roll across the top, pressing firmly to seal in the filling. Cut out the ravioli with a crimped-edge ravioli cutter.

Bring a large pot of salted water to a boil. Drop the ravioli into the water and cook until the ravioli float to the top, about 10 minutes. Drain. Serve the ravioli covered with the Marinara Sauce.   *Serves 4 to 6.*

PENNE WITH PEPERONCINI & OLIVES

2 tablespoons fresh basil
$^1/_2$ cup + 1 tablespoon olive oil
$^1/_4$ cup butter
$^1/_4$ cup minced garlic
2 cups peperoncini
1 cup sliced black olives
1 cup sliced green olives
1 cup chopped sun-dried tomatoes
1 pound penne pasta
Salt and pepper to taste
Grated Romano cheese

I prepare this dish for the members of my family who like a lot of zip in their pasta! Its rich and tangy blend of peperoncini, assorted olives, sun-dried tomatoes, and garlic is sure to delight all of your spicy-food-loving guests.

Put the basil and the 1/2 cup of olive oil in a blender and blend until a smooth paste is formed. Using a spatula, empty the contents of the blender into a large, deep skillet. Add the butter and heat up this mixture.

Add the garlic, peperoncini, black olives, green olives, and sun-dried tomatoes. Cover and simmer this mixture until the peperoncini begin to puff up and all the ingredients and their flavors have blended together well.

Meanwhile, fill a large pot with water and the remaining tablespoon of olive oil, and bring to a boil. Add the pasta and cook al dente. Rinse, and drain in a colander.

Place the hot pasta in a large serving bowl. Pour the ingredients in the skillet over the pasta and mix well. Season with salt and pepper. Serve along with a bowl of freshly grated Romano cheese. *Serves 6.*

Pasta is love!

SHELLS WITH CORN SAUCE & PANCETTA

1 pound pancetta (Italian bacon)
6 large ears fresh corn
¼ cup olive oil
2 tablespoons butter
1 large green bell pepper, chopped
1 large red bell pepper, chopped
1 medium onion, chopped
1 tablespoon minced garlic
½ tablespoon oregano
½ tablespoon basil
1 ½ cups half & half
Salt and pepper to taste
1 pound shells pasta

When I was a little girl and my mother was ill, my aunt kept me with her for a time on Mott Street in the Little Italy section of Manhattan, New York. She let me stay with her in her deli all day, which I loved, because I loved to meet and talk to all the people who came in. But she also taught me some dishes that my own mother didn't make. This dish is one of them. Just thinking about the dish makes me remember the love and kindness she gave to me during that time, so many years ago.

The pasta in this dish is called "conchiglie" because they are shaped like small conch shells.

Fry your bacon in a skillet until crispy but not too brown. Drain on paper towels, crumble, and set aside.

Using a sharp knife, cut the fresh corn kernels off each ear of corn. Cream the corn in a food processor or blender. If you use frozen corn, use about a pound, and be sure that it is completely thawed before you put it in your food processor or blender.

Heat the olive oil and butter in a large, deep skillet. Add the peppers, onion, and garlic, and sauté lightly. Before this is completely cooked, add the creamed corn. Stir in the oregano and basil. Cover, and simmer for 20 minutes.

Stir in the half & half and season with salt and pepper. (Allow the cream to blend with the corn and heat up well, but be sure not to boil or the cream will coagulate.)

Bring a large pot of water to a boil, add a teaspoon of olive oil, and cook the pasta shells al dente. Drain in a colander and serve covered with the corn sauce, and a nice handful of bacon pieces.

Serves 4.

NOTE: We prefer to do this dish in the summer months when the corn on the cob is in season and is so fresh and sweet. However, you can do the same dish with frozen corn any time of the year.

My son Neil and me in the kitchen.

MANICOTTI

MANICOTTI CREPES

If you've never had homemade manicotti crepes, you just don't know what you're missing. They're delicate, delicious, quick and easy to make, and a whole different experience than the processed manicotti shells you buy at the market. This is one of the very few dishes that I prepare in which processed Mozzarella cheese is better to use than fresh. Even though you can't beat the fresh cheese for flavor, the consistency is usually too soft for this dish and will make the filling too runny.

SAUCE

2 quarts Marinara Sauce (see page 164)

PASTA

2 cups flour
¼ cup olive oil
2 large eggs
2 cups water
⅛ teaspoon salt

This pasta is thin like a crepe, so the batter is thin as well. Combine the pasta ingredients in a large mixing bowl and beat until smooth.

Heat a crepe pan or an 8-inch skillet. (If the skillet isn't hot enough, the batter will stick.) Lightly coat with olive oil. (If you use too much oil, the batter will not spread thinly and evenly.) You should have to oil the skillet only after every 3 to 4 crepes. Ladle a small scoopful of the batter into the center of the pan and spread it evenly over the whole pan by lifting and turning the pan. The batter will spread over the pan easily because it is very thin.

Cook over medium heat until the crepe changes color and starts to curl up around the edges, about 2 to 3 minutes. You won't need to turn the crepe over—the batter is so thin that it will easily cook throughout. Use a spatula to gently loosen the manicotti crepe from the pan and lift. If the crepe sticks to the skillet

when you try to remove it, it is not done. Cool on waxed paper that you've spread over your kitchen counter.

FILLING

2 pounds Ricotta cheese
3 eggs
½ cup chopped fresh parsley
Salt and pepper (a pinch of each)
1 cup grated Romano cheese
½ pound shredded Mozzarella cheese

In a large mixing bowl, whip the Ricotta cheese with the eggs until smooth and creamy. Stir in the remaining ingredients and set aside.

ASSEMBLY

Preheat the oven to 325°F.

After you've finished cooking all the pasta crepes and they have cooled, fill each one with a heaping tablespoon of the Ricotta cheese mixture. Fold one half of the crepe over the middle, then the other half over as well. Cover the bottom of a large baking dish with about 1/2 inch of the Marinara Sauce. Retain enough sauce for drizzling over the top of the manicotti before you put them in the oven. Line up the manicotti next to each other in a large baking dish and drizzle sauce over the top of each one. Bake for 20 minutes.

Makes about 18 manicotti.

VARIATION

DESSERT CREPES: The pasta recipe above can be used for a sweet dessert crepe. Simply add 3 tablespoons of sugar and 1 teaspoon of cinnamon to the mixture. Prepare the crepes the same way as above and fill with your favorite fruits, topped off with either whipped cream or ice cream. These dessert crepes are so delicious and look so beautiful that they always impress my family and guests. And yet they are so simple and fast to make. The perfect dessert!

HOMEMADE PASTA

In our style of cooking, pasta is very similar to pizza dough in that you have your basic pasta recipe that you can change in many ways—simple ways— that change a dish very dramatically. You can add different combinations of herbs, spices, or flavorings to your pasta dough. You can add spinach, which is popular these days. (The consistency for spinach pasta is very hard to get right. If you enjoy a challenge, give it a try.) Add sugar and cinnamon and you have a sweet pasta dough for dessert dishes. Add minced garlic, parsley, and a little pepper and you have a wonderful-tasting pasta. Add a bunch of ground, crushed hot peppers, fresh basil, along with some salt and pepper, and you have a very spicy and delightful pasta. Add saffron, salt, and pepper and I guarantee your success. And then come your sauces or toppings!

When it comes to the pasta course, there are endless delicious possibilities!

Johny "Twin" and some of Neil's friends.

BASIC PASTA DOUGH

4 cups all-purpose flour

1 teaspoon salt

4 eggs

1 tablespoon olive oil

Sift the flour and salt together and pile on a pastry or cutting board. Make a well in the center and place the eggs and the oil in it. Work the eggs and oil into the flour with your fingers until a firm dough is formed. Knead the dough until very smooth and elastic, about 10 minutes. Cover the dough with a cotton cloth and let it rest for 1/2 hour. Divide the dough into 3 pieces. Roll out each piece as thin as possible on a floured board—the thinner the better. Cut as described below, depending on what type of pasta you intend to make.

Bring a large pot of water to a boil, add a tablespoon of oil, and throw in the fresh pasta. Stir the pasta immediately to make sure it is all separated. Because it is fresh, it will tend to stick together. It will take only a few minutes to cook.

FOR FETTUCCINE: Roll out the dough thinly and fold over in an accordion-type pleat, each flap being about 2 fingers wide, until the entire flattened piece of dough is folded in accordion pleats. Cut off each end so that both ends are even. With a sharp kitchen knife, cut off 1/4-inch pieces. Unfold each fettuccine strip, toss them gently (flour your hands), and lay them out on paper towels to dry for a while.

FOR SPAGHETTI: Same as above, but cut the pieces much thinner, perhaps 1/8 inch wide.

FOR SPAGHETTINI OR ANGEL HAIR PASTA: Same as above, but cut in much thinner strips—as thin as you can possibly cut them and have them stay together.

FOR LASAGNA: Prepare the same as above, but cut the pieces about 4 inches wide.

There are so many different ways to create a pasta dish. A leftover roast chicken or duck can be shredded and served on your favorite pasta with a rich brown sauce, using stock, butter, flour, and herbs. I have included many of my family's favorite pasta and sauce recipes throughout the book. Below is a list of some ingredient combinations to tickle your imagination.

1. Shredded roasted chicken, sautéed chopped onions, and minced garlic in a pesto sauce.

2. Sautéed spicy Italian sausage slices and chopped onions in a creamy marinara sauce with half & half.

3. Steamed scallops with sautéed sliced mushrooms and onions in a creamy pesto sauce (see page 162) using half & half.

4. Steamed broccoli florets, sautéed sliced mushrooms and onion, and minced garlic in a creamy wine sauce using white wine, butter, half & half, grated Romano cheese, salt, and pepper.

5. Minced anchovies, chopped sun-dried tomatoes, minced garlic, and chopped green and black olives in olive oil, salt, and pepper.

6. Steamed and chopped fresh spinach, olive oil, onions, capers, salt, and pepper.

The block in Little Italy where I raised my family had everything. The bakery was on the corner—Mammanon and I went there every morning to get fresh bread for our families. Right next to that was the candy store, then Frank the barber. Next was a little wood craft shop—they sold fancy mirrors in very beautiful, scrolled frames. Right next to that was the tuxedo shop, which is very important, because every Italian man has to have a tuxedo to wear to weddings!

Next door, Jay the butcher had his shop. And I lived with my family right above Joe the shoemaker, who was next door to the butcher. Right across the street, at the beginning of the next block was the fish market and directly across the street from the fish market was the vegetable market. Mammanon and I used to shop there every day. We bought just a little at a time—some tomatoes, a couple of cucumbers, a good onion, a head of lettuce. That way you don't waste anything, and everything is fresh. And, of course, Mammanon and Poppanon's deli was not far down the street.

Once a year in our neighborhood we have a special feast—we've been doing this as long as I can remember. For several nights the main street is closed to traffic. All the neighbors and the shopkeepers come out into the street and feast together. There are games and rides for the kids, and mountains of food for everyone. Since there are people in the neighborhood whose families come from all parts of Italy, it is a good time to taste all the different varieties and styles of Italian cooking. (Just the smell of all the different delicious foods is mouth-watering!)

This feast got started as a way to raise money for our church, and now we look forward to it each year as a time for the whole neighborhood to get together, to enjoy one another, to catch up on what is happening with everyone, and to eat a lot of different kinds of fantastic Italian food!

NEAPOLITAN RISOTTO

Most of my family's dishes are pretty simple to make. This dish is a little more complicated, but it is one of the dishes I remember my mother made most often for special occasions. The end result will impress your family and guests—trust me!

SAUCE

1 large onion
1 teaspoon minced garlic
2 tablespoons olive oil
1/4 pound mushrooms, washed and thinly sliced
6 cups crushed tomatoes
1 cup red wine
1 teaspoon basil
2 teaspoons brown sugar
1 1/2 teaspoon salt
1 teaspoon pepper
2 cups frozen peas, thawed

In a deep skillet or pot, sauté your onion and garlic in the olive oil over medium heat until the onion is tender, being careful not to brown. Add the mushrooms, sauté for a few more minutes, then add the tomatoes, red wine, basil, sugar, salt, and pepper. Cover, and simmer for about 30 minutes over low heat.

Add the peas, remove the cover, and simmer over a slightly higher heat for another 10 minutes. The sauce should be thick, not runny.

THE RISOTTO AND POLPETTE

3 cups white rice, uncooked
1 1/2 pounds ground beef
Olive oil
1 1/2 cups Italian bread crumbs, seasoned
2 large eggs
1/4 cup chopped fresh parsley
Grated peel of 1 lemon
1/4 teaspoon nutmeg
1 teaspoon minced garlic
1 teaspoon salt
1/2 teaspoon pepper
Enough flour to coat patties
Enough vegetable oil for frying
1 pound bacon
1/2 cup Italian bread crumbs, seasoned
1 pound Mozzarella cheese, shredded

FOR THE RICE: In a large pot, combine the rice with just enough olive oil to coat the grains. Sauté the rice over medium heat just long enough to get it hot, being careful not to brown the rice. Cover the rice with 1 1/2 inches of water and bring to a boil. As soon as it starts boiling, cover tightly and turn down the heat very low. Simmer until light and fluffy, about 15 minutes. (Don't take

the cover off before the 15 minutes is up, though, because the steam will escape and the steam is what cooks the rice so nicely.)

FOR THE POLPETTE (MEAT PATTIES): Put the ground beef in a large mixing bowl and combine well with the bread crumbs, eggs, parsley, lemon peel, nutmeg, garlic, salt, and pepper. Form into small patties, about 1/4 inch deep and about 1 1/2 inches wide. Coat each patty in flour, then fry in hot vegetable oil over medium heat, until golden brown. Set them aside on paper towels to drain.

Fry the bacon until golden brown and crisp. Drain and cool on paper towels. Preheat the oven to 350°F.

ASSEMBLY

Coat the bottom of an oblong baking dish with olive oil. Sprinkle and coat the dish with the bread crumbs. Spread half of the cooked rice evenly on top, then spread all of the beef patties on top of the rice. Lay the strips of bacon evenly across the patties. Spoon half of the sauce evenly over this, then half of the Mozzarella cheese. Cover with the rest of the cooked rice, then the rest of the sauce, then the rest of the cheese. Bake for 30 minutes. Let settle slightly before serving it in slices.   *Serves 6 to 8.*

PASTA WITH CREAM SAUCE & WALNUTS

1 pound mostaccioli pasta (large macaroni)
1 cup green onions, chopped
1 tablespoon minced garlic
1 tablespoon olive oil
1 cup chopped walnuts
12 ounces cream cheese (or mascarpone, if you can find it)
1 cup half & half
1/2 cup grated Romano cheese
Salt and pepper to taste
Pancetta (optional)

When I was young and my mother taught me to make this dish, we always used mascarpone, which is a very rich, creamy cheese originally from northern Italy. It's getting harder to get here these days, but if you ever come across it, don't hesitate to buy some. Even though the texture is very much like cream cheese, which works just as well in this dish, the flavor is out of this world!

Bring a large pot of water to a boil, add about a teaspoon of salt, and cook the pasta al dente.

In a medium-size saucepan, sauté the green onions and garlic in the olive oil over low heat. Add the walnuts and sauté for another

minute. Be very careful not to brown this mixture. Remove from the heat.

In a small bowl, blend the cream cheese with the half & half until smooth. Add this to the sautéed onion mixture, and mix well. Simmer for 5 minutes, stirring constantly. (This is more to heat the sauce and blend the flavors than to actually cook the sauce.) Pour this mixture into the pasta, which has been rinsed and drained. Add the grated cheese, and salt and pepper and blend well with the pasta. Serve immediately.

I sometimes will sprinkle some crisp bits of Italian bacon over the top of this dish. Either way, this is a very rich and delicious dish.
          Serves 4.

RICE CASSEROLE

2 cups white rice

2 bunches green onions, chopped

3 medium zucchini squash,
   chopped

$\frac{1}{4}$ cup butter

$\frac{1}{4}$ cup olive oil

7 eggs

2 cups grated Romano or
   Parmesan cheese

1 teaspoon salt

$\frac{1}{2}$ teaspoon pepper

$\frac{1}{2}$ cup Italian bread crumbs,
   seasoned

This dish has a rich and delicate flavor, and makes a very nourishing main course. Or you can cut it up in cubes and serve it with toothpicks as an antipasto.

Bring 4 cups of water to a boil in a large pot. Add the rice and stir. As soon as the rice begins to boil, cover and turn down the heat very low. Let simmer until light and fluffy, about 20 minutes. Set aside to cool. Preheat the oven to 350°F.

In a skillet, sauté the chopped onions and zucchini in the butter and olive oil until they are tender. Be sure not to brown the onions.

Whip 6 of the eggs in a large mixing bowl. Add the rice and grated cheese. Be sure the rice is not too hot or it will harden the eggs. Stir in the sautéed vegetables, salt, and pepper.

Oil a large glass baking dish. Coat with the Italian bread crumbs and spread the rice and vegetable mixture evenly in the dish. Whip the last egg in a small mixing bowl and, using a pastry brush, brush the egg evenly over the top of the rice. Bake until golden brown, about 45 minutes.

Cool for 1/2 hour, cut into squares, and serve. This mixture can be made ahead of time, frozen, then thawed out and baked.

Serves 4 to 6.

That's me, in 1951, standing in front of a car parked outside my apartment.

ORECCHIETTE ALLA SALSA DI CAROTE PICCANTE

PASTA IN CARROT SAUCE WITH SAUSAGE

When my mother made her carrot sauce, she always told me that before tomatoes were "invented" in Italy, our ancestors considered this sauce as basic to their cooking as marinara or meat sauce is today. I found out later that apparently there are many versions to the story about who actually brought the first tomato to Italy and when. When I was growing up I remember seeing women in the neighborhood make a similar sauce using different types of squash, even pumpkin. But my family always prepared it with carrots, I think because Mammanon believed that carrots were good for your health. I'm sure you will find this dish delicious and unusual.

1 recipe Spicy Carrot Sauce (see page 162)
4 large eggs
3 cups all-purpose flour
$^{1}/_{2}$ teaspoon salt
Grated Romano cheese

Prepare the carrot sauce with sausages.

In a medium-size mixing bowl, stir the eggs, flour, and salt together until a smooth, bread-dough consistency is formed. If too dry, add another egg. My mother never used water to moisten her pasta dough. She preferred—and I do also—to use eggs to create a rich pasta dough.

Knead the dough on a floured baking board for a few minutes, until elastic and smooth. Roll into cylinders about 1 inch in diameter. Cut tubes into 1/2-inch pieces with a knife.

Press your thumb into each piece to make an indentation like the inside of a hat. (Some people in the neighborhood refer to this pasta as "ears," but my family has always referred to them as "the hats." Set all the pieces aside to dry until you are ready to cook them.

Bring a large pot of water to a boil, add a tablespoon of olive oil, and cook the pasta noodles for 5 minutes. Turn into a colander to drain. Transfer the pasta to individual plates, top your "hats" with the sauce, and serve along with some freshly grated Romano cheese.   *Serves 4 to 6.*

RICOTTA-STUFFED PASTA

4 cups all-purpose flour

½ teaspoon salt

4 tablespoons butter

4 large eggs, whipped

1 pound Ricotta cheese

2 large eggs

1 cup grated Romano cheese

¼ pound Mozzarella cheese,
  shredded

1 cup chopped black olives

½ cup capers

½ cup chopped parsley

1 teaspoon salt

½ teaspoon pepper

2 egg whites

1 recipe Marinara Sauce
  (see page 164), optional

This is an unusual pasta in that it is baked, not boiled. The cheese filling in this recipe can be replaced by any number of meat or seafood fillings. When I make passerotti for a meal, I like to make half of them with the Ricotta mixture and half of them with leftover spicy Italian sausages from my meat sauce.

Sift the flour and salt together in a mixing bowl. Cut the butter into the flour mixture until the flour is of a mealy consistency. Pour the 4 whipped eggs over the flour mixture. Mix well with your hands, kneading the dough until it is firm but not sticky. Form into large balls for rolling.

Roll the pasta out into a thin sheet. Using a pastry cutter or knife, cut the dough into 2-inch strips, then the strips into 3-inch rectangles.

Preheat the oven to 350°F.

In a mixing bowl, blend the Ricotta with the 2 eggs and Romano cheese. Add the Mozzarella cheese, olives, capers, parsley, salt, and pepper and stir well.

Spoon a tablespoon or so of the filling into the center of one of the pasta rectangles. Place another rectangle on top and, using a fork, seal the two rectangles around the edges. Place all the filled and sealed rectangles side by side on an ungreased baking sheet.

In a small mixing bowl, whip the egg whites until they are somewhat stiff. Using a pastry brush, brush the stuffed pasta rectangles with the egg. Bake until golden brown. Serve them hot and crispy from the oven, or serve them with Marinara Sauce.

Serves 4 to 6.

STUFFED RICE BALLS

This method of cooking white rice, once mastered, produces light and fluffy rice every time, but be sure to not take the lid off the rice, which releases the steam before it is done. The steam is the secret to a nice fluffy rice.

RICE

4 cups long grain white rice, uncooked

2 tablespoons olive oil

Place the rice and olive oil in a large saucepan and add enough olive oil to coat all of the rice. Heat up the rice slightly, but do not brown. Cover the rice with 1 to 1 1/2 inches of water. The rice will sizzle when the water is being poured over it. Bring to a boil, cover, and turn down the heat. Simmer 20 minutes, then set aside.

FILLING

Olive oil for frying

1 cup chopped onion

⅛ cup minced garlic

1 pound ground beef

3 cups Marinara Sauce (see page 164)

2 cups frozen peas

1 ½ cups grated Romano cheese

2 eggs

1 pound Mozzarella cheese, cubed

Italian bread crumbs, seasoned

Heat a tablespoon or so of olive oil in a large skillet. Add the onion and garlic, and sauté for a few minutes. Be sure not to brown. Add the ground beef and brown with the onion. Add the Marinara Sauce and simmer for 20 minutes. Add the frozen peas and cook for 10 minutes. The sauce must be of a very solid consistency to be used to stuff the rice balls, so check the amount of moisture and continue to simmer to cook off the moisture, if necessary. Cool the sauce before you use it.

Put the cooked rice into a mixing bowl. Add the grated cheese while the rice is still hot, and mix well into the rice. Let the rice cool somewhat, then blend in the eggs. When the rice is cool enough to handle, scoop a small handful of the rice mixture into the palm of your hand and form a ball. Press 2 fingers into the ball, making a deep indentation. Fill with a few cubes of Mozzarella cheese and a small amount—a tablespoon or so—of the sauce. Reform the rice ball around the cheese and sauce (the mixture should be completely covered with the rice ball). Roll the balls in the bread crumbs until completely covered. Repeat until all the rice balls are formed.

In a deep skillet, heat 2 cups of olive oil. Place the rice balls in the hot oil and fry until golden brown. You may want to reserve some Marinara Sauce to drizzle over the balls before you serve them, along with a sprinkling of grated Romano cheese. I like to serve them like that.

Serves 6.

There's my daughter Annette and my niece Rosemarie in their First Holy Communion dresses. Mammanon, standing in the middle, looks just as mischievous as they do!

GNOCCHI DI RICOTTA
RICOTTA GNOCCHI

2 pounds Ricotta cheese

2 eggs

4 cups flour

2 teaspoons salt

1 teaspoon pepper

Creamy Pesto Sauce (see page 162)

1 cup grated Romano cheese

You won't be able to eat much of this rich dish at one time, but I promise you that you will savor every bite!

In a large mixing bowl, mix the Ricotta and eggs. Gradually add the flour, salt, and pepper. Knead well on a floured board. Roll into finger-size rolls and cut into pieces about 3/4 inch long.

Bring a large pot of salted water to a boil. Add the gnocchi, stirring gently from time to time to make sure they are separated. Cook for 10 minutes, then drain. You can serve them either immediately with your favorite sauce and topped with freshly grated cheese, or my favorite way:

Preheat the oven to 350°F. Spread out the cooked gnocchi in a large glass baking dish, and top them with Creamy Pesto Sauce. Sprinkle the top with a cup of grated Romano, then bake for 10 minutes, until the cheese is a golden brown.

Serves 6.

FUSILLI DELLA RUSSO

FUSILLI WITH SHRIMP & VEGETABLES

1 pound fusilli pasta
½ cup + 1 tablespoon olive oil
1 pound jumbo shrimp
1 cup chopped spinach
2 large carrots, julienned
2 large zucchini, julienned
2 large yellow squash, julienned
2 tablespoons minced garlic
½ cup chopped fresh parsley
Salt and pepper to taste

Fusilli is my son Neil's favorite pasta of all, but the fusilli that I use is a little different than most fusilli you see in the market. The kind I use is over a foot long, so long that each noodle curves into a large, curly horseshoe shape. The kind you commonly find at the market is much shorter—so keep your eyes open for the long Italian-style fusilli in specialty stores or well-stocked delis.

Bring a large pan of water to a boil. When it is at the boil stage, put a tablespoon of the olive oil in it and cook the fusilli pasta al dente. Drain, rinse, and let drain again in a colander.

While the pasta is cooking, bring another large pan of water to a boil. Cook the shrimp in the water until they turn a bright orange, about 3 minutes. Remove from the water and drain.

Heat the remaining olive oil in a large skillet. Add the vegetables and sauté lightly over medium heat. The vegetables should remain somewhat firm. Add the garlic and parsley, and sauté only long enough for the flavors to blend. Remove from the heat.

In a large mixing bowl, combine the warm pasta with the sautéed vegetable mixture. Toss in the shrimp and season with salt and pepper. You may want to add extra olive oil. Serve warm.

Serves 4.

MILANESE RISOTTO

1 cup chopped onion
2 tablespoons minced garlic
½ cup butter
2 cups white rice
1 cup Marsala wine
Chicken broth
1 teaspoon saffron
½ cup grated Romano cheese
Salt and pepper to taste

Because my family comes from a coastal region of Italy, we usually have this rice dish with some type of seafood. I like to serve it with one of my Seafood Marinara dishes (see page 74), but it's also terrific with my Lemon Chicken (see page 115).

Sauté the onion and garlic in one half of the butter in a large saucepan. Add the rice and continue to sauté, stirring constantly. Cook it just long enough to heat the rice, making sure not to brown it. Add one half of the wine and enough chicken broth to cover the rice mixture by 1 inch. Cover, bring to a boil, then immediately turn down the heat very low. Let the rice simmer about 15 to 20 minutes, depending on the type of rice you use. You want the rice to be light and fluffy, not sticky.

Meanwhile, bring the rest of the butter, wine, and the saffron to a boil in a small saucepan, and set aside. When the rice is done cooking, uncover and stir in this mixture, along with the grated cheese. Season with salt and pepper, and serve along with your favorite main course.

Serves 4.

RICE SANDWICHES

2 cups uncooked white rice
4 tablespoons butter
1 cup chopped onion
3 cups chicken broth
3 cloves garlic, minced
1 teaspoon salt
½ cup chopped fresh parsley
4 eggs
1 ½ cups grated Romano cheese
1 pound Mozzarella cheese
2 cups Italian bread crumbs,
    unseasoned
Olive oil for frying

These little sandwiches make a delicious meal along with a nice salad. They work well as an appetizer too.

In a large saucepan, combine the rice, butter, onion, chicken broth, garlic, and salt, and bring to a boil. Cover, and turn down the heat very low. Simmer until the rice is light and fluffy, about 15 to 20 minutes. Remove from the heat and mix in the parsley, 2 egg yolks, and the grated cheese. Set aside.

Flour a baking board and turn the rice mixture onto it. Pat the rice out flat, until it is about 1/4 inch thick. Let this stand until it is completely cold.

Using a round cookie cutter, cut the rice into circles. Slice the Mozzarella cheese into thin, round pieces and place between two rice pieces.

In a mixing bowl, beat the 2 egg whites with the remaining 2 eggs. Dip each rice sandwich in the egg mixture, then coat it evenly with the bread crumbs. In a medium-size saucepan, heat the olive oil until it is hot, and fry each rice sandwich until golden brown on each side.

Drain on paper towels and then put the sandwiches in a warm oven until you are ready to serve them.   *Serves 4.*

That's my father Rocco, or Poppanon, and my mother Christina, or Mammanon. They taught me all I know about great Italian cooking. That's my younger brother Tony in uniform. It's 1944, during the war, and they're standing in front of our home in Brooklyn, on the corner of 69th Street and 14th Avenue.

PIZZA

This is my basic dough recipe, but I often substitute ingredients, depending on the toppings I want to use or how thick I want to make the pizza crust. When I make a hearty, Sicilian pizza, with lots of meats, I often substitute finely ground polenta or corn meal for half of the flour. I often add herbs as well, like oregano, basil, even sage or fennel. Adding a healthy tablespoon of minced garlic is always popular in my family. And instead of the sugar, I will add more salt and a liberal amount of pepper. You can even add crushed hot red peppers for a spicy crust. Be sure to experiment with the flavors of your crust, not just your toppings.

BASIC PIZZA DOUGH

2 ¼ cups all-purpose flour
1 heaping teaspoon dry yeast
1 teaspoon sugar
¾ cup warm water
1 tablespoon olive oil
1 teaspoon salt

Put the flour in a pottery-style or metal bowl that is large enough for the dough to rise in. In a smaller mixing bowl, combine the yeast, sugar, and warm water. When this starts to fizzle, add the oil and salt. Pour this mixture into the flour, blend well, and knead in the bowl for a few minutes.

Cover with a dry dish towel and put either on top of a hot oven, inside a warm one, on a hot radiator, or in front of a lit fireplace.

(My mother had a coal stove in the back room of her deli, and I can still remember smelling her pizza dough as soon as I walked into her store.) Let the dough rise for a few hours. It should at least double in size, or even triple. If you use polenta meal in your dough, however, it will not rise quite as much.

Turn the dough out onto a floured baking board and knead a little bit. Unless you are an experienced pizza maker and can do all that fancy tossing and stretching of the dough, I suggest either rolling it out flat with a rolling pin or just shaping it into your pizza pan with your fingers. Always oil your fingers with a little olive oil when shaping into your pizza pan this way. This recipe makes one large or two thin pizza crusts.

PIZZA ALLA BRUKLINESE

1 recipe basic pizza dough
½ cup + 1 tablespoon minced garlic
½ cup olive oil
1 ½ cups chopped onion
1 teaspoon oregano
1 teaspoon basil
1 teaspoon salt
¼ teaspoon pepper
1 cup grated Romano cheese

This pizza is made for garlic lovers! We like a thick Sicilian-style crust for this recipe.

Make the pizza dough, adding 1 tablespoon of the garlic when you combine the yeast mixture with the flour. Preheat the oven to 375°F.

Heat the olive oil in a small saucepan and add the remaining garlic, the onion, oregano, basil, salt, and pepper.

Sauté over low heat until the onions are clear, making sure not to brown the onion and garlic. Roll out the dough until about 1/2 inch thick and the size of a large pizza pan, and spread the sauce evenly over the top. Bake for 15 to 20 minutes. Remove from the oven, sprinkle evenly with the grated cheese, then return to the oven and bake for another 5 to 10 minutes, until the cheese is a light golden brown.

PIZZA OREGANATA

This delicious pizza is best with a thin, Neapolitan-style crust.

½ recipe basic pizza dough
1 cup thick Marinara Sauce (see page 164)
½ pound peperoni, thinly sliced
½ pound prosciutto, julienned
1 ½ cups shredded Mozzarella cheese
2 ½ cups Italian bread crumbs, seasoned
½ cup olive oil

¼ cup minced fresh parsley
1 tablespoon oregano
1 teaspoon pepper
¾ cup grated Romano cheese
2 eggs
¼ cup minced garlic

Preheat the oven to 375°F. Roll out your pizza dough until about 1/4 inch thick and spread the Marinara Sauce over it evenly. Cover with the peperoni and prosciutto

slices, and sprinkle evenly with the Mozzarella cheese. Bake for 15 minutes.

In a small mixing bowl, combine the remaining ingredients with the tips of your fingers until the mixture is well blended but still crumbly. Remove the pizza from the oven and cover evenly with the topping. Bake for another 10 to 15 minutes, until the top and the crust are a nice golden brown.

SECONDO
MAIN COURSE

During a big Italian meal, a couple of hours can go by before you reach the main course. And there is a reason for that—the main course is the high point of the meal. You have to be prepared to appreciate it! Antipasti, soup, pasta, a little wine, some good conversation—they set the stage for the masterpiece, the real substance of the feast. And when it is time for the main dish, it is always presented alone, as a dish that is proud to be on its own. You might add a little garnish to dress it up, but that is all.

Once you have presented the main course, you might bring out a salad or vegetable dish. But never let them steal the show from your main course!

So what is the main course? There are many different foods that can be prepared as a main course. That is why this section is the largest one in this book. A main course can be a meat, poultry, or fish dish, or eggs and vegetables, but in our family, more often than you might think, the main course is seafood.

PESCI
SEAFOOD

My non-Italian friends are often surprised when they find out how often I prepare seafood as a main course. And I learned from the best—Mammanon was a real expert at preparing delicious seafood. There is a good reason for this. There are sixteen regions in Italy, and only three of them are inland. That means that thirteen regions are right on the coast. In fact, no point in Italy is more than 150 miles from either the Adriatic or Mediterranean Sea. So seafood is abundant everywhere.

Mammanon showed me many tricks from the Old Country, traditional ways to prepare seafood. One of her secrets, one that many Italian cooks use, was to combine fresh seafood with olive oil, wine, herbs, and vegetables—and to cook them together. That way, the seafood flavor becomes part of the sauce, and the flavors of the sauce become part of the seafood. It is delicious! She also taught me to combine more than one type of seafood in a dish—often fish and shellfish are cooked together in the same dish.

CARNI E POLLAME
MEATS & POULTRY

When she came to America, Mammanon had to adapt the cooking she had learned in Apulia to a new set of circumstances. One of the things she had to face was that the variety of seafood available in New York was not as great as in Apulia. But the good news was that there was a greater variety of affordable meats available in America than in Apulia. Italy does not have the vast grazing lands of America to feed cattle: land is used for growing fruits, vegetables, wine grapes, and olive trees. So, although veal (which doesn't require so much grazing space) is common in Italy—so much so that it could be considered the national meat—Mammanon found more variety at her butcher shop in New York than she could in Italy.

Because of this, many of the recipes Mammanon passed on to me used traditional Italian techniques but called for the meats available in the new world. In America, Italians like to eat a lot of the same meats and poultry as all other Americans. It's only our ways of cooking them that are different. So, enjoy the recipes in this section —they are the taste of the Old World adapted to the New!

UOVE E VERDURE
EGGS & VEGETABLES

As Italians, we cook eggs differently than most Americans. For us, eggs are not a breakfast food. As my son Neil says, "Eating eggs for breakfast was a learning experience for me, and I'm still not inclined to do it. Elodia raised me on breakfasts of a fresh roll and steamed milk with coffee (only a taste of coffee in the milk when you are young, and then more as you get older). To this day, that sounds more like breakfast to me than eggs." Instead, we like to eat eggs as a main course at lunch or dinner, usually in the form of many types of frittata, the Italian version of omelet.

There are two things I especially like about making a frittata—with an abundance of fresh meats and vegetables to choose from, you can be endlessly creative with them and, best of all, they are very quick to make. Using your leftovers or starting from scratch, you can whip up a delicious frittata in your skillet in fifteen minutes. What could be a quicker and, at the same time, more delicious main course?

Some tips: Never fold your frittata in half the way you might with an omelet. Also, never cook your frittata over a high flame, because you'll burn the bottom and the eggs will get tough. Cook it in a covered pan over low heat. That way, it comes out light and fluffy.

SEAFOOD MARINARA
MUSSELS · CLAMS · CRAB · LOBSTER

These seafood dishes are such easy dishes to prepare—and as basic to our style of cooking as any pasta dish. It's one of the dishes that my son Neil asks for the minute he gets off the plane to visit me! He says that when he thinks about having this dish at home his taste buds start getting excited! I think the real secret to this dish—and all Italian cooking—is the freshness of the ingredients. And in this case, it's also the richness of the marinara sauce. In my family, a seafood marinara sauce can't be too thick, too rich, or too spicy; however, some fish marinara dishes do better than others with a healthy dose of hot peppers or picante sauce in them. You should experiment to see which ones you like mild and which you like hot.

2 pounds mussels/clams/crab/or lobster

• • •

8 cups Marinara Sauce (see page 164)
1 cup minced onion
¼ cup minced garlic
1 teaspoon olive oil
Hot chili peppers (optional)
½ cup red wine
1 teaspoon fresh oregano
1 teaspoon basil (fresh if possible)
2 cans tomato paste
Salt and pepper to taste
1 teaspoon brown sugar (optional)

In a large saucepan, heat the Marinara Sauce over medium heat. It's best to start with a sauce that you've previously made, so that it's had time for all the flavors to blend.

While you're heating your sauce, sauté the onion and the garlic in the olive oil, being careful not to brown the mixture. (If you'd like a spicier sauce, mince a few red, green, or yellow hot peppers and sauté them with the onion mixture as well. ALWAYS USE RUBBER GLOVES WHEN CHOPPING HOT CHILI PEPPERS.) Add this sautéed mixture to your Marinara Sauce and stir in the red wine, oregano, basil, and tomato paste. Bring the sauce to a boil, cover, and reduce to a simmer for 1/2 hour. Add salt and pepper. (Some people like to throw in a pinch or two of brown sugar. It helps get rid of some of the acidity of the tomato paste. Try it to see how you like it.)

COZZE ALLA MARINARA
MUSSELS MARINARA

1 tablespoon olive oil
⅛ cup minced garlic
Pinch of oregano
Pinch of basil
1 loaf of Italian bread, thickly sliced

Buy the mussels tightly closed. If any of them are not, throw them away. Scrub them in cold water with a stiff brush and put them in a pan with 1/2 inch of water. Cover tightly and heat over high heat until all the shells have opened— about 3 to 5 minutes. Shake the pan occasionally to make sure the mussels are cooked evenly.

In a medium-size skillet, heat a small amount of olive oil with the garlic, oregano, and basil—freshly chopped if you have the herbs. Stir and lightly sauté, being careful not to brown the mixture. Lay the slices of Italian bread in the pan and fry until golden brown on both sides. Arrange a few pieces of the toast along the edge of each dish of mussels you plan to serve. Place the steamed mussels in the center of the dish and drizzle the sauce (the spicier the better for the mussels) over the insides of the mussels and over the garlic toast.

VONGOLE ALLA MARINARA
CLAMS MARINARA

Buy the smallest and the freshest clams you can find. The smaller they are, the more tasty and sweet. Scrub them first under running water with a stiff brush, then soak them in a cold-water bath for an hour or so before cooking them.

After the clams have soaked, throw them, shells and all, into your pot of sauce. Cook over medium heat for about 5 minutes, until the clams open and are tender but not chewy. Serve them over a bed of your favorite pasta. I like to use linguini. (The clams give the sauce such a wonderful flavor that usually I don't use hot peppers in my marinara with clams.)

GRANCHIO ALLA MARINARA
CRAB MARINARA

Use precooked crab meat and add it to the pot of seafood marinara sauce. Simmer just long enough for the crab flavor to permeate your sauce, about 5 to 10 minutes. I serve the crab marinara just like the clams, over a good al dente pasta. Try it with a thin pasta, like angel hair or spaghettini.

ARAGOSTA ALLA MARINARA
LOBSTER MARINARA

To save time, you can add precooked lobster meat to the pot of sauce, and cook just like the crab. If you use lobster tails, take your scissors and snip and remove the soft underside of the tails. Be sure to remove intestinal veins. Preheat the oven to 350°F. Arrange the lobster tails in a baking dish. Cover them liberally with the sauce, and bake for 20 minutes. Serve them next to a bed of fluffy rice. Drizzle the sauce over the rice as well.

Each recipe serves 4.

ARAGOSTA FARCITA
STUFFED LOBSTER TAILS

6 fresh lobster tails
½ cup diced onion
2 stalks celery
½ cup sliced mushrooms
¼ cup minced garlic
½ cup olive oil
2 cups chopped tomatoes
½ cup dry white wine
1 teaspoon Worcestershire sauce
¼ cup chopped fresh parsley
2 cups Italian bread crumbs,
   seasoned
2 egg yolks
Salt and pepper to taste

Lobster is one of the most delicious and rich of all the seafoods. This dish really shows off its wonderful taste. It has a very aromatic sauce and a bread crumb topping—between the lobster, the sauce, and the topping, you get three different ways to enjoy the lobster flavor!

Have your butcher clean and open your lobster tails. If you do this yourself, take your scissors and snip and remove the soft underside of the tails. Be sure to remove intestinal veins. Remove the lobster meat, chop, and set aside.

Wash each lobster shell well in cold water and arrange them in a baking dish.

Preheat your oven to 350°F.

Sauté the onion, celery, mushrooms, and one half of the garlic in 3 tablespoons of the olive oil for about 5 minutes, being careful not to brown the vegetables. Add the tomatoes, lobster meat, wine, Worcestershire sauce, and parsley, and simmer for 10 minutes. Season with salt and pepper, and remove the pan from the heat. Fill each tail liberally with this mixture.

Moisten the bread crumbs with the remaining olive oil. Mix in the egg yolks and the remaining garlic. Season with salt and pepper, then cover the stuffed lobsters with the bread crumb mixture. Put the stuffed tails back into the baking dish and bake for 15 minutes, until the bread crumb mixture is golden brown.

Serves 4 to 6.

MERLANGO AL ROSMARINO
ROSEMARY LING COD

1 large leek, chopped
2 tablespoons olive oil
3 large cloves garlic, minced
½ pound tomatoes, chopped
½ cup white wine
2 teaspoons fresh rosemary
1 pound ling cod
Salt and pepper to taste

This is a very tasty dish, and because of its delicious natural sauciness, it's an excellent dish to serve on a bed of fluffy rice.

In a large, deep skillet, sauté the leek in the olive oil for 5 minutes. Add the garlic, tomatoes, wine, and rosemary, and simmer for 10 minutes.

Cut the fish into small chunks and add to the mixture. Cover, and simmer for another 15 minutes. The cod will turn white and flake with a fork. When it's done, season with salt and pepper.

Serves 2 to 4.

Here's my older brother Jimmy and his wife Anna on their wedding day.

CALAMARI RIGANTE

1 pound fresh calamari
2 large eggs
1 cup flour
Olive oil for frying
1 large onion, minced
3 large cloves garlic, minced
1 cup sliced mushrooms
1/4 teaspoon chopped red chilies
6 cups tomatoes, chopped
1/4 cup chopped fresh parsley
1 heaping tablespoon fresh oregano
1/2 cup red wine
Salt and pepper to taste

This is the calamari dish that I make most, and it is a real trademark of my family's cooking style. It's quick and easy to make, and I use it sometimes as a main course, the centerpiece of the meal, and sometimes I serve it as an antipasto dish before a seafood meal.

Soak and clean the calamari in a bath of cold water and salt. Sometimes the calamari will have come from the fish market already in pieces and completely cleaned—this is preferable. If you have to do the cleaning yourself, the salt-water bath will loosen any skin left on the calamari and make it easy to remove. Pull the head away from the body, removing all the insides, including the thin cartilage backbone. Cut the tentacles off just above the eyes, but save them because they are delicious fried. After you pull the fins and skin off of the body, you will be left with a pinkish-white triangle-shaped sock. Rinse these socks inside and out under the faucet. Cut them into 1/2-inch pieces and drain. They will look like rings.

In a small mixing bowl, beat the eggs until they are frothy. Dip each piece of calamari in the egg, then roll it in the flour. In a large skillet, heat some olive oil and lightly brown the calamari pieces. (Be sure not to cook them too long or the calamari will be tough.) Drain on paper towels and set aside.

In another large saucepan, sauté the onion and garlic in about a tablespoon of olive oil. Add the mushrooms and the red chilies. Squash the tomatoes through a colander and add these and the juice from them to this mixture. Add the parsley and oregano, and simmer for 15 minutes.

Add the wine and simmer, covered, for another 15 minutes. Season with salt and pepper, add the calamari, and simmer for no more than 5 minutes. Serve with your favorite pasta.   *Serves 2 to 4.*

NOTE: Instead of rolling the calamari pieces in the egg and flour, you can simply brown the pieces in olive oil and cook in the sauce. Either way, your family won't be able to get enough of this dish once they've tasted it!

OYSTERS TETRAZZINI

4 dozen small oysters
4 tablespoons butter
4 tablespoons olive oil
1 cup Italian bread crumbs, seasoned
1/2 cup freshly grated Romano cheese
1/4 cup flour
1/2 teaspoon salt
1/2 teaspoon pepper
1/2 teaspoon paprika
1 tablespoon Worcestershire sauce
3 cups milk
1/4 cup Marsala wine
1 pound flat egg noodles

When preparing this dish, remember: the smaller the oyster, the more flavorful this dish will be.

Have the fish market remove the oysters from their shells and give you the shells (for decoration later) in a separate container. Be sure they also reserve the oyster juice in a separate container for you. When you get home, rinse the oysters well, being careful to strain out any pieces of shell.

In the top of a double boiler, melt the butter with the olive oil. Take half of this and mix with the bread crumbs and the cheese. Set aside. Whisk the flour, salt, pepper, paprika, and Worcestershire sauce into the remaining butter and oil in the double boiler. Whisk in 1/2 cup of the oyster juice and the milk. When smooth and thick, whisk in the Marsala. Remove from the heat.

Preheat the oven to 350°F.

While you are cooking the sauce, bring a large pot of salted water to a boil. Cook the noodles al dente, rinse, and drain.

Place the noodles in a baking dish. Pour one half of the sauce over them and stir well. Arrange the oysters over the top of the noodles, cover with the rest of the sauce, and sprinkle evenly with the bread crumb mixture. Bake for 1/2 hour.

Serve on individual plates, surrounding each portion with the reserved oyster shells, covering the shells half way with the pasta.
                    Serves 4 to 6.

TIELLA BARESE
BARI'S VERSION OF PAELLA

This is an old family dish that comes originally from Bari, Italy, where my father was born.

FILLING

$\frac{1}{2}$ pound bacon (or pancetta)

$\frac{1}{4}$ cup olive oil

1 cup chopped onions

$\frac{1}{8}$ cup minced garlic

$\frac{1}{2}$ cup sliced celery

4 cups diced red potatoes

$\frac{1}{2}$ cup sliced mushrooms

3 cups chopped clams

In a skillet, brown the bacon. Transfer to paper towels to drain, reserving the fat in the skillet. Add the olive oil and sauté the onion and garlic in this for a few minutes. Add the celery, then the potatoes. Continue sautéing over medium heat until the potatoes are tender. Add the mushrooms and clams, cover, and simmer for 10 minutes over very low heat.

Remove from the heat and pour the mixture evenly into a lightly oiled, glass baking dish. Crumble the bacon over the top. Set aside.

SAUCE

$\frac{1}{2}$ cup butter

3 tablespoons all-purpose flour

1 cup milk

1 cup half & half

1 teaspoon paprika

1 tablespoon chopped fresh parsley

Salt and pepper to taste

Melt the butter in a small saucepan over low heat. Gradually stir in the flour, being careful not to brown. Slowly stir in the milk, then the half & half and paprika. Stir continuously until the sauce begins to thicken. Add the parsley, and season with salt and pepper. When the sauce is sufficiently thick, remove from the heat and pour evenly over the dish.

TOPPING

3 cups Italian bread crumbs, seasoned

1 cup grated Romano cheese

$\frac{1}{4}$ cup chopped fresh parsley

$\frac{1}{4}$ cup minced garlic

$\frac{1}{2}$ cup olive oil

2 eggs

Preheat the oven to 350°F.

Combine all of the ingredients in a mixing bowl. The mixture should be moist but have a slightly mealy consistency. Cover the top of the baking dish with the topping, pressing it into the potato-clam mixture and sauce.

Bake for 20 to 25 minutes, long enough for the topping to be golden brown. Serve with a fresh salad. *Serves 4.*

PESCE ALLA LIGURE
FISH IN SPICY SAUCE

$\frac{1}{2}$ pound mushrooms

2 pounds fish steaks (whiting, ling cod, or tuna)

2 tablespoons olive oil

1 tablespoon minced garlic

4 anchovy fillets, chopped

2 tablespoons all-purpose flour

1 $\frac{1}{2}$ teaspoons salt

$\frac{1}{4}$ teaspoon crushed chili peppers

$\frac{1}{2}$ teaspoon pepper

2 cups dry white wine

$\frac{1}{4}$ cup chopped fresh parsley

2 tablespoons lemon juice

I usually do this recipe with a whiting or a light-colored fish. If you can get a fresh piece of tuna (tonno) from your meat market, this is a delicious fish to use in this recipe too.

Wash the mushrooms well in a bath of cold, salted water. Drain and slice. Wash and drain the fish.

Heat the olive oil in a large, deep skillet. Stir in the garlic, mushrooms, and anchovies. Then stir in the flour, add the salt, chili peppers, pepper, and wine, and stir until smooth. Cover, and simmer for 5 minutes.

Cut the fish into serving-size slices and add to the sauce. Sprinkle with parsley and lemon juice, and cover. Simmer for about 15 to 20 minutes, or until the fish is tender and flaky.

Serve the fish on a bed of white rice. Drizzle some of the spicy anchovy and mushroom sauce over the rice as well.

Serves 4.

CHRISTMAS EVE FEAST

CHRISTMAS EVE FEAST

TRADITIONALLY, FOR ITALIANS, BOTH CHRISTMAS EVE AND CHRISTMAS DAY ARE MAJOR FEASTS. And so, for a few days, it seems like there's cooking going on day and night. Usually, all the women in the family get together in the kitchen—between sisters, cousins, nieces, aunts, great aunts, mothers, and grandmothers, there are a lot of us in there! Often, there are three generations of women cooking together—there's always a lot of laughter and talk, a lot of catching up on gossip, and sharing of cooking methods. It is a wonderful time, one that I love.

Of all our feasts, though, I think Christmas Eve is my favorite. For Mammanon and for me, there is a religious background to this dinner—it is a meatless meal, made entirely of seafood dishes. For us, and for many Italians, it is a religious observance to abstain from meat as Christmas approaches. But, at the same time, for everyone, our seafood feast on Christmas Eve celebrates the holiday season in a very festive way. It is an old Italian tradition, one that Poppanon and Mammanon brought with them from the Old Country.

When you see a spread like the ones Mammanon and I have always prepared for Christmas Eve dinner, it's easy to appreciate the fact that in Apulia, where she was born and where she learned to cook seafood so well, many people eat seafood more often than they eat meat. I remember many times Poppanon, and then my husband, and then my son going crabbing off the New York coast, or going down to Coney Island to get big, black mussels off the rocks. It was a lot of fun for them, but I always felt that doing that was a link to our Italian roots. They were collecting the local seafoods for our table, just like Poppanon's father did in Italy, and his father before him.

That is why, at Christmas Eve dinner, Mammanon used to serve between ten and fifteen different kinds of seafood dishes. And they were dishes that were traditionally served on Christmas Eve when she was growing up in Apulia. They are all dishes that "you have to have," as she used to tell me.

My son Neil and my daughter Annette visiting with Santa Claus. Neil looks pretty confident, but Annette is not too sure. At Christmas, we prepare one of our biggest feasts—maybe Neil is old enough to remember all the good food and the gifts that are about to come.

So, in our Christmas Eve dinner, even the antipasti includes a lot of seafood. Next comes the pasta dish. That is the one part of the Christmas Eve meal that I vary—for example, if I made manicotti at Thanksgiving, or even more recently, for someone's birthday, then I would make lasagne or some other type of pasta dish. But I would always also include a pasta dish like spaghetti or linguini with some kind of seafood sauce.

Then comes the main course. These dishes include every kind of seafood—like shrimp oreganata, mussels marinara, stuffed calamari, baked clams, stuffed fish, as well as crab and lobster and many other seafood dishes. Then there are the vegetable dishes and salads that we serve on the side. And, finally, there are all kinds of special Christmas desserts: anisette cookies, cannoli, ricotta pie, struffoli, all served with espresso and liqueurs.

As you can see, Christmas Eve dinner is one of the most elaborate feasts of the year. But don't forget that on Christmas Day itself, there is another feast, this time with turkey, ham, leg of lamb, or roast chicken, and no seafood. That is why we used to say, "At Christmas time, you eat for a week!" (And if you don't actually eat enough to keep you from getting hungry for a week, you will certainly have enough delicious leftovers to last you that long!)

When I was growing up, and when my kids were growing up, we always celebrated Christmas Eve at Poppanon and Mammanon's. In the afternoon, while the food was cooking, the whole family got together in the living room to decorate the tree. Candles were always burning, the decorations were all put out, and the nativity scene was set up under the tree. During our Christmas Eve get-together, everyone was always excited and happy; there were always lots of hugs and lots of gifts, in addition to all the food.

Today, some people ask me why I still make Christmas Eve dinner such an elaborate affair. What can I say? It's the family tradition. Besides, can you think of anything better to do at Christmas than to get the whole family together for a feast like this one?

SALMONE NATALIZIO
CHRISTMAS EVE ROAST SALMON

1 cup butter
1 cup olive oil
2 cups thinly sliced onion rings
1/2 cup minced fresh basil
1 tablespoon fresh rosemary
1/4 cup minced garlic
1 teaspoon salt
1/2 teaspoon pepper
1/2 cup fresh lemon juice
1/2 cup capers
1 fresh salmon (8 pounds)
Thin lemon wedges or rings
   for garnish

Because all of the dishes for our traditional family Christmas Eve feast are seafood, we always like to find a big, fresh fish to roast and decorate for the centerpiece of the table. Although you could roast many types of fish using this recipe, I like salmon best.

Preheat the oven to 400°F.

Melt 1/4 cup of the butter with 1/4 cup of the olive oil in a deep skillet. Add the onion, and sauté over medium heat until the onions begin to become clear.

Add the remaining butter and olive oil and melt the butter. Stir in the basil, rosemary, and garlic. Sauté this mixture for a few minutes, then add the salt, pepper, and lemon juice. Simmer for a minute or so, then add the capers.

Rinse the salmon and lay it in a roasting pan large enough for the fish to be completely in the pan, fins and all. Pour the onion mixture over the salmon and bake 40 to 50 minutes, basting regularly. If you keep the fish covered with the sautéed onions they will help to keep the fish moist.

Remove the fish from the oven when it flakes when tested with a fork. Transfer to a heated platter and lay all the onion slices across the fish as well. Garnish with the lemon slices.

ANGUILLA ALLA MAMMANON
MAMMANON'S EEL DISH

Everyone in my family advised me not to include this recipe in my cookbook, but how could I not have it in my cookbook? These days, it's only in the old, old families that you can still get eel dishes. When I was growing up, they were as normal to my parents' table as pizza is to my grandchildren's today.

2 pounds eel
1 cup flour
1 teaspoon salt
1/2 teaspoon pepper
1/4 cup olive oil
1/4 cup butter

Cut the eel into 1 1/2 to 2-inch pieces. (Be sure you purchase your eel already skinned and washed well. Particularly if this is the first time you've had eel, you just don't want to go through that part of the process!) In a medium-size mixing bowl, combine the flour, salt, and pepper, and roll the eel in the mixture. In a skillet, heat the olive oil and butter over medium to high heat and fry the eel until well browned. Set aside to drain on paper towels.

SAUCE
1/8 cup olive oil
1/2 cup minced onion
1/8 cup minced garlic
1 1/2 cups chopped tomatoes
2 tablespoons tomato paste
1 tablespoon minced parsley
1 teaspoon basil
1 cup chicken broth
1/2 teaspoon salt
1/2 teaspoon pepper

Heat the olive oil in a deep skillet. Sauté the onion and garlic, but be sure not to brown them. Add the tomatoes and blend in the tomato paste. Stir in the parsley, basil, chicken broth, salt, and pepper. Cover, and simmer for 20 minutes over medium heat. Add the drained eel to this sauce, cover, and continue to simmer for another 15 minutes. Serve with a nice pasta. *Serves 4.*

RISOTTO DI CAPESANTE
SCALLOPS & RICE CASSEROLE

1/4 cup olive oil
1 pound large fresh scallops
2 large onions, chopped
1 large green pepper, chopped
2 large stalks celery, chopped
1/2 pound mushrooms, chopped
3 large cloves garlic, minced
2 pounds fresh tomatoes
1/2 teaspoon dried oregano
1/2 teaspoon dried basil
1 teaspoon salt
1/2 teaspoon pepper
1 1/2 cups uncooked rice

There are two different types of scallops that you can get. The kind you more commonly find at the market is processed and shaped into small chunks. I like the fresh scallops. They come in very thin pieces that are ruffled, or "scalloped," along the edges, and they are so much more tender and delicious, they are definitely worth searching for.

Preheat the oven to 350°F. Heat one half of the olive oil in a large, deep skillet, and sauté the scallops on both sides for about 5 minutes. Transfer the scallops to a large casserole dish. Place the remaining olive oil in the skillet and sauté the onions, green pepper, celery, mushrooms, and garlic. Add the tomatoes and tomato juices, which have been squashed through a colander, and bring to a boil. Add the oregano, basil, salt, and pepper. Stir in the rice and remove from the heat. Pour the mixture over the scallops and mix well. Cover, and bake 45 minutes. *Serves 4.*

CALAMARI FARCITI
STUFFED CALAMARI

1 pound calamari

2 ¹/₂ cups Italian bread crumbs,
  seasoned

¹/₄ cup minced garlic

¹/₄ cup minced fresh parsley

³/₄ cup grated Romano cheese

2 eggs

¹/₂ cup olive oil

Salt and pepper to taste

6 cups Marinara Sauce (see page 164)

Traditionally, this calamari dish is always served on special occasions or holidays. We always have it for our Christmas Eve feast. You can make it with either the mild or the spicy version of the Marinara Sauce.

You can either purchase your squid fully cleaned or not. They are pretty easy to clean yourself, and usually quite a bit cheaper. To clean the squid, hold each one in a sink full of cold water while you peel off and discard the thin outer skin. Cut off the heads just below the eyes. You can either discard the tentacles or keep them to bread and fry later for your appetizers. Squeeze out the insides and discard the transparent, thin bone. Each calamari will look like a pinkish-white wind sock, the wide end open and ready to stuff. Wash them again in cold water and set aside to drain.

Preheat the oven to 350°F.

In a separate mixing bowl, combine the bread crumbs, garlic, parsley, grated cheese, eggs, and olive oil. Season with salt and pepper. The mixture should be slightly mealy but hold together if you squeeze it in the palm of your hand. Stuff each calamari about half-way full, using your fingers to stuff the mixture well into each calamari sack. (When the calamari cook, they blow up, so you can't fill them too full with the stuffing or they will open up and let the stuffing out.) Close each calamari with a toothpick, as if you were stitching the calamari with a needle. Line up the stuffed calamari pieces in a baking dish and pour the Marinara Sauce over them liberally, covering them with the sauce. Cover tightly with foil and bake for about 30 minutes. They should be tender but not rubbery from overcooking.

Serve your favorite pasta either on the side or under the stuffed calamari and sauce.

Serves 4.

GAMBERONI IN PANCETTA
PRAWNS WRAPPED IN PANCETTA

½ pound pancetta (unsmoked Italian bacon), cut in very thin strips
2 pounds jumbo prawns
½ cup butter
½ cup olive oil
Juice of 4 lemons
¼ cup minced garlic
¼ cup minced fresh parsley
¼ cup minced black olives
Salt and pepper to taste

For this dish, find out where the best fish market near you is and get the plumpest prawns they have. Even if you have to go a little farther, it's well worth it—there's just no comparison to the freshest of seafood!

Wrap the strips of bacon around the prawns and fasten with toothpicks. Melt the butter in a large, deep skillet and add the olive oil. Sauté the bacon-wrapped prawns on both sides until they turn a nice bright pink and the bacon is crisp. (Be sure not to overcook the prawns or they will be tough.)

Line up the prawns on a serving platter and remove the toothpicks. When the prawns are cooked properly the bacon will adhere to them naturally.

Stir the lemon juice and garlic in the skillet with the olive oil, butter, and bacon drippings. Add the parsley and olives, season with salt and pepper, then dribble this sauce all over the wrapped prawns. Serve while they are nice and hot. *Serves 4.*

SEAFOOD OREGANATA
MUSSELS · CLAMS · SHRIMP · LOBSTER

These are very special seafood dishes to our family. We always serve at least one of them, sometimes several, with our traditional Christmas Eve seafood feast. And believe it or not, they are simple as can be to prepare. You just make one big batch of the bread crumb stuffing, and take it from there. I'm getting hungry writing about them!

STUFFING

2 ½ cups Italian bread crumbs, seasoned
¾ cup grated Romano cheese
¼ cup minced garlic
½ cup olive oil
2 eggs
1 tablespoon minced fresh oregano
½ cup minced fresh parsley

Mix all of the ingredients together in a mixing bowl. The mixture should have a somewhat mealy consistency but be moist enough to hold together if you squeeze some in the palm of your hand.
Makes enough for 2 pounds of fish.

There's Annette at her "sweet sixteen" party with her proud mother (me) in our apartment in the early 1950s.

COZZE OREGANATE
MUSSELS OREGANATA

VONGOLE OREGANATE
CLAMS OREGANATA

Buy the mussels or clams tightly closed. If any of them are not, toss them out. (Be sure to purchase the smaller clams—they're always tastier.) Scrub them under cold water with a stiff brush and soak them in a bath of cold, salted water for an hour or two.

Rinse the mussels or clams, then put them in a pan with about an inch or so of water. Cover them tightly and heat over high heat until all the shells have opened, about 3 to 5 minutes for most varieties of mussels and the smaller varieties of clams. Shake the pan occasionally to be sure they are cooking evenly. Save the water and clam juice mixture (or mussel juice) and drain the shellfish.

Arrange the steamed shellfish in a lightly oiled baking dish. Spoon a little of the steaming juice into each shell, and stuff each shell with a heaping teaspoon of the stuffing mixture. Dribble some of the steaming juice around the stuffed shells in the baking dish, then broil until the stuffing begins to turn a golden brown, about 3 minutes. Serve immediately.

SCAMPI OREGANATI
SHRIMP OREGANATA

Buy the plumpest, freshest jumbo shrimp at your market. Clean them well under cold running water, and drain. Preheat the oven to 350°F. Oil a baking dish lightly with olive oil. Arrange the shrimp in the dish and spread the stuffing mixture evenly over the top of the shrimp. Bake for 15 to 20 minutes. The shrimp should be tender and juicy, and the stuffing crisp and golden brown.

ARAGOSTA OREGANATA
LOBSTER OREGANATA

I always use fresh lobster tails for this dish. One tail is usually enough for one serving—depending on your appetite! But this is such a luscious dish, you just might need two.

Soak the tails for an hour in cold, salted water. Using scissors, snip off the soft underside shell. Make sure you remove the intestinal vein. Rinse the tails well under cold, running water. Preheat the oven to 350°F.

Lightly oil a baking dish with olive oil. Arrange the tails in the dish and pack the stuffing down around the inside of and on top of the meat of the tail—as much as you can get in. Place about 1/2 inch of water in the baking dish without getting the stuffing wet or damp—this will make it too soggy. Bake 15 to 20 minutes, until the tails are tender when tested with a sharp knife, and the stuffing is crispy and golden brown. *Serves 4.*

RED SNAPPER & GREEN SAUCE

1 slice Italian bread
1 cup olive oil
½ cup lemon juice
⅛ cup minced fresh parsley
⅛ cup minced garlic
1 tablespoon minced fresh basil
½ teaspoon sugar
½ teaspoon salt
½ teaspoon pepper
½ cup minced green bell pepper
2 tablespoons capers
4 to 6 red snapper fillets

This is a very tangy, light, and fresh-tasting dish. It works great for a healthy and fast meal after a busy day.

Place the bread slice, olive oil, lemon juice, parsley, garlic, basil, sugar, salt, and pepper in a blender and blend well. If it's too thick, add equal amounts of olive oil and fresh lemon juice. Pour this into a mixing bowl and stir in the green pepper and the capers.

Lay the fillets in an oiled baking dish and cover with the green sauce. Get your oven good and hot on broil and broil the fillets for 10 minutes. Serve while hot. *Serves 4.*

STUFFED TROUT

4 trout (8 to 10 ounces each), cleaned
½ cup olive oil
½ cup chopped onion
½ cup chopped celery
¼ cup minced garlic
2 ½ cups Italian bread crumbs, seasoned
¼ cup minced parsley
2 heaping tablespoons ground sage
½ cup pine nuts
¾ cup grated Romano cheese
½ teaspoon salt
½ teaspoon pepper
2 eggs

This is another of my family dishes that I often serve as part of our Christmas Eve seafood feast (see page 85).

Brush the trout liberally with olive oil and lay them in a baking dish. Preheat the oven to 400°F.

Heat the olive oil in a skillet, and sauté the onion, celery, and garlic over medium heat until the onions are clear. Be sure not to brown the mixture. Transfer this to a mixing bowl and add the bread crumbs, parsley, sage, pine nuts, grated cheese, salt, and pepper. Using either a fork or the tips of your fingers, mix in the eggs.

Fill each trout's cavity with the stuffing—but not so full that you would need to tie them. Bake for about 20 minutes, or until the trout meat flakes when punctured with a fork. Garnish with sprigs of fresh parsley.

Serves 4.

My aunt Cora and her husband "Red" in front of their house on 14th Avenue in Brooklyn, in 1951.

FRIED CALAMARI WITH GARLIC SAUCE

If you cook calamari too long, or even not long enough, they will tend to be rubbery in texture. But if you cook them just right, they are tender and absolutely delicious. If you start with the freshest calamari you will find you've won half the battle, and you are in for a great treat!

1 $\frac{1}{2}$ pounds calamari

2 eggs

$\frac{1}{2}$ cup + 2 tablespoons olive oil

2 $\frac{1}{2}$ cups Italian bread crumbs, seasoned

$\frac{1}{4}$ cup minced parsley

$\frac{3}{4}$ cup grated Romano cheese

$\frac{1}{4}$ cup minced garlic

$\frac{1}{2}$ teaspoon salt

$\frac{1}{4}$ teaspoon pepper

If your market hasn't cleaned the fish for you, hold each one in a sink full of cold water while you peel off and discard the thin outer skin. Cut off the heads just below the eyes and discard. (Some of my family members like the tentacles breaded and fried along with the regular calamari meat—it's a matter of taste. Squeeze out the insides of the fish and discard the inside transparent thin bone. The calamari will look a little like a small version of those wind socks that some people put on their boats and porches. Wash them well in cold water, then cut them into rings about 1/2-inch wide.

In a small mixing bowl, beat the eggs until frothy. In another mixing bowl, combine 1/2 cup olive oil with the bread crumbs, parsley, grated cheese, garlic, salt, and pepper. Heat a tablespoon or two of olive oil in a frying pan. Dip each piece of calamari in the beaten eggs, then roll in the bread crumb mixture. Fry in the skillet until golden brown, about 3 minutes. Transfer pieces to paper towels to drain until all the pieces are fried.

SAUCE

1 cup olive oil

2 tablespoon fresh lemon juice

$\frac{1}{4}$ cup minced garlic

3 egg yolks

1 tablespoon dark mustard

$\frac{1}{2}$ teaspoon salt

1 teaspoon basil (fresh, if you have it)

$\frac{1}{2}$ teaspoon oregano

$\frac{1}{2}$ teaspoon thyme

$\frac{1}{2}$ teaspoon sugar

Blend all the ingredients in a high-speed blender until creamy. Depending on how much of a garlic lover you are, you may want to play with the amount of garlic you use until you get it just right. For a spicier sauce, add 1/8 teaspoon of cayenne pepper. Serve the fried calamari pieces with the sauce either dribbled over them or on the side to dip the pieces into. *Serves 4.*

FISH WITH MUSHROOMS

2 to 3 pounds cod, halibut, or
  sole, cut into pieces
1 cup all-purpose flour
2 teaspoons salt
1 teaspoon pepper
1/2 cup + 3 tablespoons olive oil
1/2 cup minced onion
1/8 cup minced garlic
2 cups sliced mushrooms
4 cups chopped tomatoes
3/4 cup chicken or fish stock
1/2 cup dry red wine
1/2 cup tomato paste
1 teaspoon basil
1/2 teaspoon oregano
1/2 teaspoon thyme
1/2 teaspoon rosemary
2 bay leaves

This dish is a wonderful meal all by itself, but it is also terrific served over your favorite pasta.

In a mixing bowl, combine the flour with 1 teaspoon of the salt and 1/2 teaspoon of the pepper. Coat the fish liberally with the flour mixture. Heat 1/2 cup of the olive oil in a skillet and sauté the fish pieces briefly and evenly on both sides until browned. Set them aside on paper towels to drain.

Heat the remaining olive oil in a large, deep skillet. Add the onion, garlic, and mushrooms, and sauté over medium heat. Be sure not to brown. Add the chopped tomatoes, stock, and wine.

Simmer covered for 10 minutes. Stir in the tomato paste. Add the basil, oregano, thyme, rosemary, bay leaves, and the remaining salt and pepper. Cover and simmer for another 20 minutes. Preheat the oven to 375°F.

Arrange the browned fish pieces in a deep glass baking dish. Pour the tomato mixture over the fish pieces and bake uncovered for 10 minutes. *Serves 4 to 6.*

SHRIMP BALLS

2 tablespoons butter
Olive oil for frying
1/2 cup minced onion
1/2 cup minced celery
1/2 cup grated zucchini squash
4 cups minced shrimp
1/4 cup minced parsley
1 teaspoon paprika
4 eggs
1 cup fine Italian bread crumbs,
  unseasoned
2 cups regular Italian bread
  crumbs, seasoned

My favorite seafood to make this dish with is shrimp, but sometimes I do the same dish with crab meat or salmon. If you really want to do something special, try it with smoked salmon or smoked oysters. It's a little expensive, but well worth it!

Melt the butter with 2 tablespoons of olive oil in a skillet, and sauté the onion, celery, and zucchini until tender. Add the shrimp and sauté for 1 to 2 minutes. Pour this mixture into a mixing bowl. Add the parsley, paprika, and 2 eggs, mix well, then blend in the bread crumbs. Shape into balls about 3/4 inch high.

That's my husband Gaetano rowing my son Neil and my daughters Annette and Marilyn in Prospect Park in Brooklyn.

Beat the remaining 2 eggs in a small mixing bowl and put the seasoned bread crumbs in another bowl. Heat a few tablespoons of the olive oil in a skillet. Dip and coat each ball in the egg mixture, then roll in the bread crumbs. Fry in the skillet over medium heat until golden brown all over. Drain on paper towels. Serve with a leafy green salad and a vinaigrette dressing, or with your favorite pasta marinara dish.

Serves 4 to 6.

SHRIMP IN CREAM SAUCE

1 medium onion, chopped

1 cup chopped tomatoes

1/2 cup grated carrot

1 teaspoon minced garlic

1 bay leaf

3 tablespoons olive oil

3 tablespoons butter, melted

1/2 cup dry white wine

1 1/2 pounds tiger shrimp

1 cup clam juice

1 teaspoon salt

1/2 teaspoon pepper

1 tablespoon lemon juice

1 teaspoon all-purpose flour

1 cup half & half

It's been passed down in our family many times—don't use milk or cream with seafood. The flavors usually don't blend well, and Mammanon used to say that they didn't sit well in the stomach. But this dish is one of her dishes that was an exception to that rule. The creamy sauce with the fresh shrimp is delicious and nourishing.

In a large skillet, sauté the onion, tomatoes, carrot, minced garlic, and bay leaf for a few minutes in the olive oil and half of the butter. Add the wine, shrimp, clam juice, salt, pepper, and lemon juice. Cover, and simmer for 15 minutes.

Remove the shrimp from the sauce and set aside. Whisk the flour and remaining butter into the sauce. Slowly whisk in the cream, being careful not to lump or curdle the sauce. Adjust the salt and pepper to your taste. Simmer over very low heat for just a minute or two, long enough to warm the cream into the mixture, stirring constantly. Pour over the shrimp and serve.

I like to serve the shrimp on top of a bed of fluffy rice, or over fettuccini with the sauce on top, but it's a nice dish to serve by itself as well.   *Serves 4.*

BROILED SWORDFISH WITH FRUIT

1/4 cup olive oil

1 cup thin apple slices

1 cup thin onion slices

2 tablespoons grated orange zest

1/2 cup dry white wine

2 tablespoons lemon juice

1/2 teaspoon sugar

1 teaspoon salt

1/2 teaspoon pepper

4 firm swordfish steaks
     (5 ounces each)

My family has always liked the unusual and tangy combination of fish and fruit in this dish. It's fresh and light, and makes a great summer dish.

Preheat the oven to 400°F.

Heat the olive oil in a deep skillet. Add the apple and onion, and sauté until the onion is tender and clear, about 5 minutes. Add the orange zest, wine, lemon juice,

sugar, salt, and pepper, and continue to sauté for a minute or so. You may want to adjust the salt and pepper.

Oil a baking dish lightly with olive oil and lay the fresh swordfish steaks in it. Pour the apple-onion mixture over the top of the swordfish steaks and broil for about 8 to 10 minutes, or until flaky when tested with a fork.   *Serves 4.*

This was a real traditional Italian wedding. I'm behind the bride, second from the left in the middle row. The flower boy on the right is my brother Tony—it's our cousin's wedding.

GIAMBOTTE
SAUSAGE, CHICKEN, PEPPERS, & POTATOES

2 pounds sweet or spicy Italian
    sausage, sliced

4 boneless, skinless chicken breasts,
    sliced

¼ cup olive oil

2 cups diced potatoes

2 cups sliced green bell peppers

1 cup sliced onion

1 teaspoon oregano

Salt and pepper to taste

In our dialect, giambotte means "mixture." It's a peasant dish, a quick and delicious way to use leftovers, and one of the dishes I remember most from my childhood. Mammanon always told me that this dish is from Bari, the town in southern Italy where my father is from.

If you use sweet sausage in this dish you may want to add hot red pepper flakes (like the ones you sprinkle on pizza) to make a spicy giambotte. If you use the spicy sausage, the dish should be spicy enough without the chilies. You know what I like to say— try it out! Experiment!

Rinse a large skillet. While the pan is still wet, put over medium heat and add the sausage. (The moisture left in the pan will bring out the sausage's natural oils, which will cut down on the olive oil you will need to use to sauté the rest of the ingredients.) Turn down the heat very low and sauté until the sausage is browned. Remove the sausage and set aside in a bowl.

Sauté the chicken pieces in the oils from the sausage in the skillet. Turn the heat down low and sauté, covered, until the chicken pieces are very tender. Transfer them to the bowl with the sautéed sausage.

In the same skillet, heat up the olive oil, and add the potatoes, peppers, and onions. Brown the vegetables over low heat. Stir in the oregano, and when the vegetables become tender, season them with salt and pepper.

Add the browned sausages and chicken, and sauté until all the flavors are mixed together and the sausage and vegetables are tender. For additional spiciness, stir in 1/2 teaspoon of hot red pepper flakes.

Giambotte is delicious heated up and made into a sandwich the following day.

Serves 4 to 6.

Starting from the left in the back, there is Mammanon, Poppanon, my sister-in-law Mary, her daughter Marie, my friend Mary Kennedy, then from the left in front, my friend Ceil, my husband, me, Ceil's husband, and my daughter Marilyn. We are all in my living room in Brooklyn, in the early 50s. I loved to cook for my family and friends at get-togethers like this more than anything!

BRACIOLE
STUFFED FLANK STEAK ROLLS

In my neighborhood in Brooklyn, and where I grew up in Little Italy, Manhattan, all you have to say to the butchers is "flank steak for Braciole," and they will know exactly how to prepare it. And if you pay extra, they will stuff it for you as well! However, there are many ways to stuff the Braciole. Italian cooks in my neighborhood add quite a variety of ingredients to the stuffing, depending on the region of Italy their family is from. I've seen some add chopped hardboiled eggs, raisins, dried figs, bread crumbs, and even "pignoli" or chopped pine nuts. My family didn't add these ingredients, but you might experiment with them to see which version suits your taste best. Either way, always use a lot of fresh garlic. Besides making the steak and its sauce taste out of this world, garlic helps to tenderize the meat.

2 pounds flank steak

3 cups grated Romano cheese

1 1/2 cups minced parsley

1 cup minced garlic

1 1/2 teaspoons salt

1 teaspoon pepper

Olive oil for frying

Brooklyn Meat "Gravy" (optional)
   (see page 158)

Cut the steak into 1/2-inch-thick slices. You don't want it too thin or it will shred too much when it is cooking in the meat sauce. Using a mallet or a meat tenderizer, pound each piece of steak until it is flat, tender, and thin, about 1/8 to 1/4 inch thick. Trim off any excess fat and set the slices of steak aside.

In a separate mixing bowl, combine the grated cheese, fresh parsley, garlic, salt, and pepper. Put a very healthy handful of the stuffing mixture in the center of each piece of flank steak and roll up each one like a small jelly roll. Tie the pieces with string so

that the rolls do not fall apart. In a skillet, brown the Braciole rolls in a very small amount of olive oil over medium heat.

If you'll be serving the Braciole as a main course, preheat the oven to 350°F. Line up the rolls in a baking dish and bake them for 1 to 1 1/2 hours, depending on the size of the rolls. When you remove them from the oven, remove the strings, and slice them in 1/4 to 1/2-inch slices and serve.

If you want to serve the rolls with the Meat "Gravy" and a pasta, and you have prepared your sauce, remove the rolls from the skillet and place them inside the pot with your sauce, along with any other meats you intend to add. Simmer this over low heat for 1 1/2 to 2 hours, or until the meats are very tender. The longer you simmer it, the richer the sauce will be. Skim off any excess oils from the top of the sauce as you simmer it. Serve the meats in the sauce by themselves, or along with a large bowl of pasta.

Serves 6.

VEAL SCALLOPINE

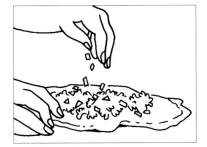

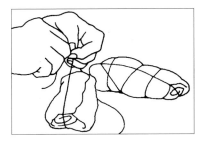

1 pound veal cutlet, cut into 6 pieces

3 tablespoons flour

1/2 teaspoon salt

1/4 teaspoon pepper

1/4 teaspoon paprika

3 tablespoons olive oil

1/2 cup minced onion

1/2 cup sliced mushrooms

1/8 cup minced garlic

3/4 cup dry white wine

2 tablespoons lemon juice

1 heaping tablespoon chopped fresh parsley

1/4 teaspoon tarragon

2 teaspoons butter

The secret to this dish is to really pound and tenderize the veal pieces. If you do, after you have cooked them in their sauce the veal will just melt in your mouth.

Pound each piece of veal until it is 1/8 to 1/4 inch thick. Sift together the flour, salt, pepper, and paprika, and coat each piece liberally with the mixture. In a skillet, heat the olive oil, and sauté a few pieces of the veal at a time on both sides until golden brown. Set aside in a place where they'll stay warm.

Add the onion, mushrooms, and garlic to the remaining hot oil in the skillet, and sauté until the vegetables are tender but not browned. Add the wine, lemon juice, parsley, tarragon, and butter, and simmer for 5 minutes. Adjust the salt and pepper to your taste. Place a cutlet or two on individual plates and top with the sauce. *Serves 2 to 4.*

POLLO ALL'APULIA
CHICKEN APULIA

1 fryer (3 to 4 pounds), cut into
 8 pieces
¼ cup olive oil
2 large eggs, beaten
1 cup flour
1 large onion, minced
2 teaspoons minced garlic
3 large stalks celery, chopped
2 cups chopped tomatoes
1 tablespoon basil
½ cup sliced green olives
1 ½ tablespoons capers
½ teaspoon sugar
½ cup dry white wine
Salt and pepper to taste

Mammanon brought this dish with her from the Old Country—it's a traditional Old World dish that originated in the region of Italy where she grew up. It is served with farfalle, bow tie shaped pasta, so it is very festive looking.

Wash the chicken pieces well and drain. Heat the olive oil in a large skillet. Dip each piece of chicken in the egg, then roll in the flour. Sauté until golden brown on both sides. (The chicken shouldn't be cooked all the way through because it will be baked later.)

Preheat the oven to 350°F.

Add the onion and garlic, and continue to sauté for a few minutes. Be sure not to brown the onion or garlic. Add the celery, sauté for a few minutes, then add the tomatoes, basil, olives, capers, sugar, and wine. Simmer for 10 minutes, then turn all ingredients into a large casserole, cover, and bake for 1 hour.

I like to serve this dish with farfalle. Put a large scoop of the chicken and vegetables in the center of the noodles, drizzle some of the sauce over the pasta, and sprinkle with some freshly grated cheese.

Serves 4.

POLPETTE DI MANZO
MEATBALLS

2 pounds ground sirloin
1 cup grated Romano cheese
½ cup chopped parsley
1 teaspoon minced garlic
2 cups fine Italian bread crumbs,
 seasoned
2 large eggs
1 teaspoon salt
½ teaspoon pepper
Olive oil for frying

If you are eating the meatballs as a main dish, rather than in a sauce, you may want to serve them with the Potatoes Oreganata (see page 141) and a salad. This makes a delicious and hearty meal. Serve the meatballs and potatoes sprinkled with some freshly grated Romano cheese.

Combine all of the ingredients in a large mixing bowl, retaining 1 cup of the bread crumbs to roll the balls in before frying.

The mixture should be solid, not mushy. If too mushy, add some more bread crumbs. Shape the meat mixture into balls and roll them in the bread crumbs, just enough to coat each ball. Set aside. The meatballs can be baked or fried. To fry, heat a small amount of olive oil in a skillet, and add the balls. Brown over low heat until the meat is cooked all the way through.

To bake, which cuts down on some of the calories and cholesterol, preheat the oven to 350°F. Lay the balls in a very lightly oiled baking dish and bake for approximately 45 minutes to an hour, depending on the size of the meatball.

Makes 10 to 20 meatballs, depending on size.

My husband Gaetano, Poppanon, my friends Jean and Bill, and Mammanon having a dinner I made in my small kitchen in Brooklyn in 1958. Even in the tiniest kitchen you can feed your family abundantly!

TIMBALLO DI MANZO
EASTER MEAT PIE

3 cups all-purpose flour

1 teaspoon salt

$\frac{1}{2}$ teaspoon pepper

1 cup grated Romano cheese

1 cup butter, softened

7 to 8 tablespoons water

$\frac{1}{2}$ pound spicy sausage, thinly sliced

$\frac{1}{2}$ pound sweet sausage, thinly sliced

$\frac{1}{4}$ pound salami, thinly sliced

$\frac{1}{4}$ pound proscuitto, diced

4 cups chopped tomatoes

$\frac{1}{4}$ cup chopped fresh parsley

$\frac{1}{2}$ teaspoon oregano

6 hardboiled eggs, thinly sliced

$\frac{1}{2}$ pound Provolone cheese, diced

This dish is what you would call a deep-dish pizza. Our family has always called this "Easter Pie" because we always serve it as one of the dishes for our Easter Sunday meal. We usually use a solid Ricotta cheese in it, but I'm told that one of the only places you can find this is in Little Italy, New York, or in my neighborhood in Brooklyn! I've tried this recipe with a good imported Provolone cheese and it works just as well.

Sift the flour, salt, and pepper together. Mix in 1/2 cup of the grated cheese. Using a pastry cutter or 2 forks, blend in the butter, creating an even, mealy consistency. Gradually blend in the water, until a large ball of pie dough is formed. Turn the dough onto a floured baking board and roll out to fit a large, deep baking dish. Press the crust into your baking dish, making sure you have a good amount of dough around the edge of the dish to shape your edges. Set aside.

Preheat the oven to 350°F.

Lightly brown the sausages in a skillet and set aside. In a mixing bowl, toss the other meats with the rest of the grated cheese, tomatoes, parsley, and oregano.

Place a layer of the sausages at the bottom of the pie shell, cover with a layer of egg slices, a layer of the chopped meats and tomatoes, then a layer of the Provolone cheese. Continue layering until you have used all these ingredients, but top off the pie with the Provolone cheese.

Bake the pie for approximately 45 minutes. Keep the light on in your oven so that every once in a while you can check to see that the cheese isn't browning and the crust isn't getting overdone. Cool slightly before serving. *Serves 6.*

A G N E L L O   P A S G U A L I N O

EASTER LEG OF LAMB

½ cup olive oil
½ cup minced garlic
½ cup chopped fresh parsley
1 cup grated Romano cheese
1 teaspoon pepper
1 leg of lamb (5 pounds), boned

The secret to making this dish tender and delicious is to cut deep pockets in the lamb, stuff them liberally, and bake the lamb slowly, basting it regularly. We traditionally serve this dish with Potatoes Oreganato (see page 141), but I also like to serve it with rice.

Preheat the oven to 325°F.

In a small mixing bowl, combine the olive oil, garlic, parsley, grated cheese, and pepper.

Cut 1-inch slits or pockets all over the piece of lamb, and fill all the slits in the meat with the garlic mixture.

Bake for 2 hours, or until the lamb is tender. Slice and serve. *Serves 6.*

Mammanon used to tell me that you couldn't have Easter Feast without lamb. "You can make your lamb a lot of different ways," she said, "but you have to have lamb."

EASTER FEAST

EASTER FEAST

FOR ITALIAN AMERICANS, EASTER SUNDAY IS A BIG CELEBRATION, as big as Christmas. But even though it's as important as Christmas, we celebrate it in a different way. On Christmas Eve, for example, we have a big feast—but not on the night before Easter. The tradition before Easter is to fast—on Good Friday, many Italian Americans don't eat meat, only seafood. And I still fast half a day on the Saturday before Easter Sunday. So, at Easter, everything points to one big day, Sunday, and the feast we have on that day.

Weeks before Easter, we get started. The ground has thawed out, so the men start preparing their backyard gardens. It's also a time for spring cleaning, airing out the house after the winter. We also shop for new clothes for everyone, including the kids. New hats for the spring are always a favorite—on Easter Sunday, everyone wants to look their best! Then, after church, it's home to prepare the feast!

The Easter feast meal is always longer than a weekly Sunday dinner—the antipasti is even more elaborate than usual, and, after the pasta course (which can vary, according to what you like), I serve a number of main course dishes. Unlike Christmas Eve, for Easter, you don't serve seafood as a main course. In fact, there is one special main course that is always served as part of the Easter feast: Mammanon used to tell me that you couldn't have the Easter feast without lamb. "You can make your lamb a lot of different ways," she said, "but you have to have lamb." She said it was "a benediction" to have lamb on the table, a symbol of the religious blessings of this time of year. We always serve the lamb dish along with a number of other main course dishes. Chicken soup with escarole and very small meatballs is another Easter favorite. And then, of course, there are vegetable dishes on the side and a big tossed salad with everything but the kitchen sink in it.

There are special Easter desserts too—like "Sweet Pie," Baba au Rum, and all kinds of cakes. But there is one special bread we

Poppanon and Mammanon receiving congratulations on their silver anniversary. They taught me so much about putting love into everything I cook. This was a very happy day, and it was wonderful to cook a feast for them just the way they taught me.

make only at Easter—it's a big, round, sweet Easter bread made from Struffoli dough (see page 176), with whole eggs baked right into it. Of course, it's very unusual to have eggs in a bread this way—they're hardboiled first, and then, when the bread dough has been formed into a wreath-like shape, a circle with a hole in the middle of it, three or four of the hardboiled eggs are pushed half way down into the top of the bread, going around the wreath. You can still see the eggs, shell and all, sticking out of the top of the loaf. It looks beautiful (see photo page 106), and when it is done it tastes delicious.

When the bread bakes, the eggs cook again— being baked this time instead of boiled. And when the bread is sliced, the egg is peeled and sliced along with the bread. Everyone gets some of the egg along with their bread and enjoys the wonderful taste of the egg (and the bread!) and the good luck that this dish is supposed to bring. Mammanon always told me that it was a good omen for the coming year to have the bread on the table as a centerpiece for Easter Sunday dinner. According to tradition, just having the bread as a centerpiece was supposed to bring luck to everyone, but Mammanon always added something extra. Right after taking the bread from the oven, she would slip a silver dollar into it. The person who got the slice with the coin in it would get *extra* good luck that year.

Everyone wanted to get that slice! My son Neil did everything he could to get that coin—he would peek, push the bread around, tell her when to cut his slice—but Mammanon was too sharp for him. Peeking was strictly against the rules! She would cut the bread the way it was supposed to be cut, everybody got their piece, and whoever was supposed to get the silver dollar— just by chance, not by fudging with the rules—got it.

Being with family and friends on Easter is always a very happy time. Everybody has new clothes, the weather is getting warm, the days are getting longer, trees are budding. In a way, this wonderful Easter feast seems more like the beginning of the year than January first.

LAMB CHOPS WITH FENNEL

1 large onion, chopped

1 heaping tablespoon minced garlic

¼ cup + 2 tablespoons olive oil

2 tablespoons butter

12 lamb chops

1 cup minced fresh fennel

¼ cup minced fresh parsley

1 cup dry white wine

3 tablespoons lemon juice

Salt and pepper to taste

Feta cheese (optional)

This dish was one of my father's favorites, one that I can still hear him requesting from my mother for dinner. The dish combines some very unique flavors, but in addition, my father used to crumble oven-warmed feta cheese on top of his lamb chops, fennel sauce, and rice. I highly recommend that you try it.

In a medium-size skillet, sauté the onion and garlic in 1/4 cup of olive oil and the butter until the onion is clear. Do not brown.

Pound and flatten the lamb chops until they are tender and approximately 1/4 inch thick.

In another skillet, brown the lamb chops on both sides in the remaining olive oil. Add the onion and garlic mixture, fennel, parsley, wine, and lemon juice. Cover, and cook over medium heat until the chops are very tender. Season with salt and pepper. You may want to thicken the sauce just a little bit by whisking a teaspoon of flour mixed with water into the sauce.

Serve the lamb chops on or next to a bed of fluffy rice, drizzle the sauce over the rice, and crumble warm feta cheese over the top, if desired. *Serves 6 to 8.*

LAMB & RICE CASSEROLE

2 pounds boned lamb

½ cup olive oil

1 large onion, chopped

2 large green peppers, chopped

1 ½ pounds eggplant, cut into cubes

2 large cloves garlic, minced

1 cup uncooked rice

5 large ripe plum tomatoes, chopped

1 cup dry red wine

1 teaspoon ground cinnamon

1 teaspoon salt

1 cup freshly grated Romano cheese

Lamb is more common in the Old Country than in America, since everyone here is more accustomed to eating beef. This dish is a wonderful way to introduce your family and friends to the Old World taste of lamb.

Cut the lamb into small cubes and brown the lamb in the olive oil. Add the onion and green peppers, cover, and cook until the vegetables are soft. Transfer to a large glass baking dish. Preheat the oven to 350°F.

In the same skillet, sauté the eggplant with the garlic until the eggplant is tender. Place this mixture over the lamb in the baking dish. Add the rice, tomatoes, wine, cinnamon, salt, and one half of the grated cheese, and blend well. Cover, and bake for 1 hour. Sprinkle the remaining grated cheese over the top before serving. *Serves 4.*

CABBAGE WITH ITALIAN SAUSAGE

2 tablespoons butter

2 tablespoons olive oil

1 pound spicy Italian sausages, thinly sliced

2 pounds cabbage, cut into strips

½ cup chopped fresh parsley

Salt and pepper to taste

We often serve this dish as a side dish at our Sunday family dinners. It could very easily be a main dish, however, and it is my favorite kind of recipe— a few fresh and tasty ingredients, fast and easy to prepare—and delicious!

Melt the butter in a large skillet and add the olive oil. Sauté the sausages over medium heat for 5 minutes. Lay the cabbage over the sausage mixture and pour 1/4 cup of water evenly over the top. Sprinkle with parsley. Stir, and cook covered over very low heat for 20 minutes. Serve immediately.

Serves 4 to 6.

DUCK CASSEROLE

1 duck (5 to 6 pounds), cut into
    pieces
2 tablespoons olive oil
½ pound prosciutto, chopped
3 large leeks, sliced
2 carrots, sliced
2 cups sliced mushrooms
3 cloves garlic, minced
2 cups dry white wine
1 cup chicken broth
1 ½ cups white rice
2 cups frozen peas
¼ cup chopped fresh parsley
Salt and pepper to taste

Italians in the Old Country like to eat all kinds of game. So even though I usually make this casserole with duck, you could make it with many other kinds of game or poultry.

Wash the pieces of duck, removing as much of the fat as possible. Drain on paper towels.

Heat the olive oil in a large skillet. Brown the duck on all sides over medium heat. Remove all the melted fat. Add the prosciutto, leeks, carrots, mushrooms, and garlic. Cover, and cook 5 minutes.

Add the wine, chicken broth, rice, peas, and parsley. Turn down the heat as low as you can, cover, and simmer for at least an hour. Don't uncover to check rice for at least 45 minutes. The rice should be fluffy and the duck pieces should be tender. Season with salt and pepper.

Serves 4 to 6.

STUFFED CORNISH HENS

20 chestnuts, unpeeled
¼ pound sliced mushrooms
    (regular or shiitake)
½ cup sliced green olives
2 tablespoons butter
½ cup olive oil
1 pound sweet Italian sausages
    (or spicy, if you prefer), sliced
1 cup coarse Italian bread crumbs,
    seasoned
4 small cornish game hens
    (1 pound each)
16 porcini mushrooms
½ pound pancetta (Italian bacon)
2 tablespoons flour
2 cups chicken broth
Salt and pepper to taste

We make this dish for special meals and holidays. You could also use this stuffing for a turkey or roast chicken. I like to roast the smaller birds because they're so tender and succulent. Serve the hens with a rich brown gravy made from the drippings, and a bowl of fluffy white rice.

Cut a slit in each chestnut and sauté in 1/4 cup olive oil over very high heat for 5 minutes. Transfer to a baking dish and bake for another 10 minutes. Remove from the oven, peel the skins from the nuts, and coarsely chop. Set aside in a mixing bowl. (If you prefer, you can use canned chestnuts, but be sure to rinse them well in cold water before you chop them.)

In a skillet, sauté the sliced mushrooms and olives in the butter and a tablespoon of the olive oil until they are tender. Add this to the bowl of chestnuts. Mix in the sausages and bread crumbs and set aside.

Preheat the oven to 350°F.

Rinse the cornish hens well in cold water, making sure everything is removed from their cavities. Stuff them abundantly with the stuffing mixture. Fasten or sew up their cavities with either poultry pins or a thick twine and carpet needle. Sometimes it works to tie the legs together with some twine. If some of the stuffing ends up dripping into the pan, it just makes for a thicker, richer gravy.

Rub olive oil all over their skin, and sprinkle liberally with salt and pepper. Wash the porcini mushrooms, remove their stems, and lay them on top of the hens. Cover the mushrooms and the entire hens with the thin layers of pancetta. Bake for an hour, basting periodically.

After they are done, spoon up the drippings into a saucepan. Whisk in the flour and the chicken broth over medium heat and continue stirring until the sauce begins to thicken. Season with salt and pepper. Serve the stuffed hens and sauce with a big bowl of rice. *Serves 4 to 6.*

STEAK PIZZAIOLA

2 pounds round, sirloin, or other
  cut of steak
2 large green peppers, sliced
1 large onion (optional), sliced in
  thin arcs
2 tablespoon olive oil
1 heaping tablespoon minced
  garlic
6 cups chopped tomatoes
½ cup chopped fresh parsley
1 teaspoon oregano
1 teaspoon salt
½ teaspoon pepper
1 cup grated Romano cheese

I will sometimes serve a nice loaf of warmed Italian bread with this dish instead of pasta or rice. My family and I love to dip the bread in the steak sauce!

Pound and tenderize the steak. It should be about 1/2 inch thick. Put the steak in a baking dish. The steak can be baked whole, or cut into pieces and spread evenly in the baking dish. Sauté the peppers and onion (optional) lightly with the olive oil and minced garlic in a skillet until they are tender.

Preheat the oven to 350°F.

Squash the tomatoes in a colander, removing and discarding the hard ends of the tomatoes and saving the juices. Mix the tomato pulp and juice with the sautéed peppers, and add the parsley, oregano, salt, and pepper. Let simmer for a few minutes. The vegetables should remain somewhat firm. Spread the vegetables evenly over the steak, cover, and bake until the steak is tender, about 45 minutes.

Serve the steak with bread or with rice, linguini, or spaghettini on the side. Spoon some sauce from the baking dish over the steak and the rice or pasta. A crisp salad will also accompany this dish when I serve it, and have a bowl of freshly grated Romano cheese on the table as well.
Serves 4.

On the right is my brother Jimmy and one of his buddies in 1944, during the war.

LEMON CHICKEN

1 chicken (4 to 5 pounds)
  cut into 8 pieces
1 ½ cups fresh lemon juice
1 tablespoon oregano
¼ cup minced garlic
2 tablespoons chopped fresh mint
¾ cup olive oil
1 teaspoon salt
½ teaspoon pepper

We make this chicken dish often in the summer months, and it can be either baked or barbecued.

Wash the pieces of chicken well in a bath of salted cold water. Drain on paper towels.

Preheat the oven to 325°F.

In a large mixing bowl, combine the lemon juice, oregano, garlic, mint leaves, olive oil, salt, and pepper and coat the chicken pieces with it well. Let marinate at least 1 hour (overnight is better).

Lay the chicken out in a baking dish, retaining the marinade for basting. Bake for 1 hour, basting periodically with the marinade. *Serves 4.*

VARIATIONS

1. Replace the fresh lemon juice and mint with red cooking wine or red wine vinegar—this creates a very different marinade, but it is equally delicious.

2. When the chicken is three fourths of the way cooked (and has been basted several times with marinade), sprinkle fine, seasoned Italian bread crumbs on top of the chicken pieces, moisten with the marinade, and bake until tender and the topping is golden brown.

CHICKEN & RICE CASSEROLE

1 chicken, cut into 8 pieces
¼ cup olive oil
2 cups rice
1 large onion, chopped
3 large cloves garlic, minced
1 pound green beans, sliced
2 pounds plum tomatoes, chopped
½ cup sliced mushrooms
½ cup chopped pimentos
½ cup chopped fresh parsley
1 teaspoon salt
½ teaspoon pepper
1 cup water
Freshly grated Romano cheese

Here's a really good candid family photo—there's my sister-in-law Anna standing behind Poppanon and Mammanon, with my nephew Rocco in front, and me, with my son Neil and my daughter Annette, on the rooftop of our apartment house in Brooklyn. We went up there often, especially on Sunday afternoons, to eat and talk and escape the heat of our apartment.

Since I don't use pimentos very often in my cooking, this dish is special. The pimentos give the chicken and rice a very distinctive flavor—something a little different.

In a large skillet, brown the chicken pieces lightly in one half of the olive oil on both sides. Drain on paper towels.

Preheat the oven to 350°F.

In the same skillet, sauté the rice, onion, and garlic in the rest of the olive oil just long enough to heat the rice. Be careful not to brown. Add the green beans and tomatoes, and simmer another 5 minutes. Add the mushrooms, pimentos, parsley, salt, and pepper, and cook for another 5 minutes.

Arrange the chicken in a large baking dish and pour the mixture over the chicken. Add the water, cover, and bake until both the chicken and rice are tender, about 1 hour. Serve sprinkled with grated cheese. *Serves 4 to 6.*

VEAL OR CHICKEN ROLLS

6 to 8 veal cutlets

2 cups fine Italian bread crumbs, seasoned

1 cup grated Romano cheese

1/2 cup chopped fresh parsley

1 cup chopped Mozzarella cheese

1 cup chopped prosciutto or salami

1/4 cup minced garlic

1 teaspoon salt

1/2 teaspoon pepper

Olive oil

I often make this dish with chicken as well. If you want to do a Chicken Spiedino, use boned and skinned chicken breast cutlets instead of the veal and prepare them the same.

Flatten out each cutlet with a meat tenderizer or mallet to about 1/4 inch thick. Preheat the oven to 350°F.

In a large mixing bowl, combine the bread crumbs, Romano cheese, parsley, Mozzarella, prosciutto or salami, garlic, salt, and pepper. Spread a layer of this mixture over each flattened cutlet. Roll up the cutlet and skewer with wooden skewers. Depending on the size of the cutlets, you may be able to fit 2 on each skewer.

Lightly coat each cutlet with olive oil. Lay them in a baking dish and bake until the meat is tender, about 1 hour. You may want to turn the skewers once or twice during the baking time.

Serves 6 to 8.

VEAL CASSEROLE

2 pounds veal

2 cups Italian bread crumbs, unseasoned

1/2 teaspoon basil

2 tablespoons minced garlic

1/2 cup freshly grated Romano cheese

2 large eggs, beaten

6 tablespoons olive oil

1 pound sliced mushrooms

1 large onion, chopped

6 cups Marinara Sauce (see page 164)

1 pound shredded Provolone cheese (imported, if possible)

This is a very rich and delicious dish. It's almost like a lasagna—but instead of using layers of pasta, you use layers of tender breaded veal. With the Marinara Sauce, Provolone cheese, and mushrooms, this dish would satisfy a king!

Pound and flatten the veal to about 1/4 of an inch thick. Combine the bread crumbs, basil (fresh, if possible), garlic, and Romano in a mixing bowl. Dip the slices of veal into the egg, then into the bread crumb mixture.

Heat 4 tablespoons of olive oil in a skillet and brown the veal on each side over medium heat. You may have to add more olive oil at times. Drain the veal on paper towels.

Preheat the oven to 350°F.

Sauté the mushrooms and onion in 2 tablespoons of olive oil and set aside.

Spread a thin layer of the Marinara Sauce on the bottom of a baking dish. Add a layer of the veal slices, then a layer of mushrooms. Top with some shredded Provolone cheese. Cover this with the sauce, then repeat all the layers until all the ingredients are used up. End with some sauce, and then shredded Provolone on top.

Cover and bake until the veal is tender, about 1 hour. Remove the top of the baking dish and bake for another 10 minutes. Be sure not to brown the Provolone on top.

Serves 4 to 5.

CHICKEN HUNTER'S STYLE

1 chicken (5 pounds), cut into pieces

¼ cup olive oil

1 cup flour

1 cup chopped onions

1 cup sliced mushrooms

1 cup julienned carrot

1 cup julienned green pepper

1/8 cup minced garlic

8 cups chopped, peeled tomatoes

½ cup tomato paste

¾ cup red or Marsala wine

1 teaspoon oregano

1 teaspoon basil

1 ½ teaspoons salt

1 teaspoon pepper

Freshly grated Romano cheese

The best cacciatora is cooked slowly for a long time, so that the flavors in the sauce are subtle and perfectly blended, and the chicken is tender as butter. Therefore even though I say to let this dish simmer for an hour, if you have the time, simmer it for two hours on very low heat.

Wash and drain the chicken pieces. Heat the oil in a deep skillet. Roll and coat each chicken piece in the flour, and brown each piece on all sides to a golden brown. Transfer the chicken to paper towels to drain.

Sauté the onion, mushrooms, carrot, green pepper, and garlic in the same skillet for 10 minutes. Add the tomatoes and sauté for another 5 minutes. Stir in the tomato paste, wine, herbs, salt, and pepper, and cook over medium heat for another 5 minutes.

Add all the chicken pieces and mix well. Turn down the heat very low, and simmer, covered, for 1 hour. Adjust the salt and pepper to your taste. Serve with some freshly grated cheese and a nice warm loaf of Italian bread. I like to dip my bread in the sauce, don't you?

Serves 4 to 6.

VEAL ROLLS WITH PROSCIUTTO

12 veal cutlets, very thinly sliced

¹/₂ cup minced garlic

¹/₄ cup olive oil

Salt and pepper to taste

2 tablespoons ground sage

1 pound prosciutto, thinly sliced

¹/₄ cup butter

1 cup dry white wine

3 to 4 fresh sage leaves, chopped

My mother used to call these "jump in your mouth" rolls. I believe that is what "saltimbocca" means literally in our dialect. And these veal rolls are so tender, aromatic, and juicy that they seem to do just that.

Flatten the cutlets as thin as possible. Combine the garlic with the olive oil in a small bowl and spread this mixture on each cutlet. Sprinkle each of them with salt and pepper, then with the sage. Top with thin layers of the prosciutto. Roll up the cutlets, and hold them together with toothpicks.

Meanwhile, melt the butter in a skillet and sauté the rolls evenly on all sides until nicely browned, about 10 minutes. Add the wine, sage leaves, and salt and pepper. Cover and simmer the rolls until tender.

You can thicken the wine sauce with just a little bit of cornstarch or flour dissolved in cold water. Adjust the seasonings and serve the rolls along with some fluffy rice with the sauce drizzled over it.   *Serves 4 to 6.*

COSTOLE ALLA FRIULANA
SPARERIBS FRIULI

¼ cup olive oil

3 pounds spareribs, cut into
   2-inch-wide pieces

1 large onion, diced

3 large stalks celery, diced

3 large cloves garlic, minced

2 large carrots, diced

¼ cup chopped fresh parsley

2 cups water

1 teaspoon ground sage

1 medium head green cabbage,
   shredded

Salt and pepper to taste

This is another of Pappanon's favorite dishes. The cabbage adds a fresh, light taste to the richness of the spareribs.

Heat the olive oil in a large skillet and sauté the spareribs on all sides. Add the onion, celery, and garlic. Sauté for 5 minutes.

Add the carrots, parsley, water, and sage. Season with salt and pepper, cover, and turn the heat down low. Simmer for 40 minutes.

Add the shredded cabbage, cover, and simmer until the cabbage is tender, about 10 minutes. Season with salt and pepper. *Serves 6.*

Some of the "girls" in the family—that's me on the right with my daughters, Marilyn and Annette, and a friend. My Aunt Cora and niece Rosemarie and friends are on the left.

STUFFED BELL PEPPERS

1 cup rice

5 large green bell peppers

3 cups Marinara Sauce
  (see page 164)

$^{1}/_{2}$ cup red wine

1 cup chopped onion

$^{1}/_{8}$ cup minced garlic

1 pound ground beef

$^{1}/_{4}$ cup olive oil

2 cups chopped tomatoes

1 teaspoon salt

$^{1}/_{2}$ teaspoon pepper

1 cup freshly grated Romano cheese

1 cup pine nuts

$^{1}/_{2}$ cup sliced black olives

$^{1}/_{2}$ cup chopped parsley

Shredded Mozzarella cheese
  (optional)

Although Stuffed Peppers is a dish that just about everyone in my neighborhood prepares, the type of stuffing changes a great deal, depending on the region in Italy ones family comes from. Even though I've tasted a lot of different stuffings made by my friends, I have always preferred the kind that Mammanon used to make. This is how she did it.

Bring 2 cups of water to a boil in a medium-size saucepan. Add the rice, turn down the heat, and cook covered for 15 minutes. When the rice is light and fluffy, set aside.

Cut off the tops of the peppers and remove the seeds. Place in a large pot of boiling water and boil until the peppers are tender but still firm. Transfer the peppers to a large colander to drain.

Preheat the oven to 350°F.

In a saucepan, bring the Marinara Sauce to a boil, then lower the heat. Add the red wine, cover, and let simmer.

In a large skillet, sauté the onion, garlic, and ground beef in the olive oil. When the beef begins to brown, add the tomatoes, salt, and pepper, and simmer for 10 minutes. Remove from the heat and stir in the Romano, pine nuts, olives, parsley, and the cooked rice. Fill each of the peppers with the mixture.

Pour the Marinara Sauce in the bottom of a baking dish. Place the stuffed peppers in the sauce. Bake for 20 minutes. If you like a more cheesy dish, after baking for 20 minutes cover each pepper with some shredded Mozzarella cheese and return to the oven just long enough to melt the cheese.

Serve the peppers on individual plates surrounded by the Marinara Sauce.

Serves 5.

A N I T R A   A L L E   O L I V E
DUCK WITH OLIVE SAUCE

1 duck (5 to 6 pounds),
   cut into pieces
3 tablespoons flour
2 teaspoons salt
1 teaspoon pepper
½ teaspoon oregano
2 tablespoons olive oil
1 cup diced onion
1 cup diced celery
2 cloves garlic, minced
1 cup red wine
2 cups chicken broth
2 bay leaves
2 cups sliced green olives

Olives and duck—these two flavors are perfect with each other. Your family and friends will remember this dish, because the flavors are so distinctive.

Wash the duck pieces well, removing as much of the fat as possible.

Heat the olive oil in a large skillet. Combine the flour, salt, pepper, and oregano. Coat each duck piece in the flour mixture, then brown on both sides in the olive oil.

Remove half of the fat and add the onion, celery, and garlic. Continue to brown. Remove as much of the fat as possible,

then add the wine, chicken broth, and bay leaves. Cover, turn down the heat very low, and simmer for 45 minutes to an hour, or until the duck is tender. Baste the duck regularly.

Add the olives. Cover, and simmer for 10 minutes over very low heat. Adjust the salt and pepper to your taste. Transfer the duck pieces to a warmed serving dish, then pour the olive sauce over the duck.
Serves 4.

FRITTELLE DI VERDURA

MINI FRITTATA

1 large onion, diced

1 tablespoon minced garlic

1/4 cup butter

1 cup diced artichoke hearts

1/2 cup sliced mushrooms

1 cup grated zucchini

12 eggs

1 teaspoon salt

1/2 teaspoon pepper

1 cup grated Romano cheese

1 cup Marinara Sauce
   (see page 164)

I used to make this frittata the usual way—in a large skillet—but one day I had my twin great-grand-daughters with me. As a treat, I baked each of them their own small frittata in my muffin pans. They were so good that way that I've made this dish that way ever since.

Sauté the onion and the garlic in the butter until the onion is clear, but be careful not to brown. Add the artichoke hearts, mushrooms, then the zucchini, and sauté for another 5 minutes. Spoon this mixture into oiled muffin tins, about half-way up.

Preheat the oven to 375°F.

Beat the eggs with the salt and pepper until frothy. Mix in the grated cheese, then pour evenly over the top of the vegetables. Top each one with a tablespoon of the Marinara Sauce and bake 15 minutes. Let cool for 5 minutes. Use a knife to loosen the edges of each frittata and serve.

Like all of our egg and vegetable dishes, they make a terrific sandwich as well.

ZUCCHINE IN UMIDO

SQUASH WITH TOMATOES, LEEKS, & EGGS

1 pound green and yellow
   zucchini squash

1 large leek

1/4 cup olive oil

1 teaspoon minced garlic

1 cup chopped ripe tomatoes

1/2 teaspoon salt

1/4 teaspoon pepper

1 teaspoon oregano

6 large eggs, beaten

1/2 cup grated Romano cheese

This is a nutritious main meal, and fast to prepare. Not only that, Mammanon would say "it's a rich man's dish on a poor man's pocket!"

Wash the zucchini, and cut the ends off. Don't peel the skin—that's where all your vitamins are. Cut into small cubes.

Wash and slice the leek into thin rings. Put all of this into a large skillet with the olive oil and minced garlic, and begin sautéing over medium heat.

Add the tomatoes (if you don't have fresh, use canned plum tomatoes), salt, pepper, and oregano, and simmer for about 15 minutes.

Combine the eggs in a mixing bowl with the grated cheese, and stir into the squash mixture. Cook, while continuously stirring, until the eggs are done. Serve immediately.   *Serves 4.*

My daughter Annette and her husband Vinny in Brooklyn on their wedding day in 1960.

VEGETABLE FRITTATA

2 tablespoons olive oil

2 tablespoons butter

$^1/_2$ cup sliced onion

1 cup sliced mushrooms

$^1/_2$ cup julienned red bell pepper

3 medium zucchini squash, julienned

1 tablespoon minced garlic

6 large eggs

$^1/_2$ cup grated Romano cheese

$^1/_4$ cup chopped chives

2 tablespoons lemon juice

2 tablespoons chopped fresh parsley

$^1/_2$ tablespoon basil

1 sprig dill

$^1/_2$ teaspoon salt

$^1/_4$ teaspoon pepper

1 cup shredded Mozzarella cheese

Frittatas can be made simply, with only a few ingredients, but I make this one more elaborate, with a lot of fresh vegetables in it. It makes a perfect meal for those evenings when you want something light and fresh, but you can't spend a lot of time preparing it.

In a medium-size skillet, sauté the onion and mushrooms in the olive oil and butter for 5 minutes. Add the pepper, zucchini, and garlic, and sauté for an additional 5 minutes.

In a separate mixing bowl, whip the eggs, lemon juice, grated Romano, chives, parsley, basil, dill, salt, and pepper. Pour evenly over the sautéed vegetables in the skillet and sprinkle with the Mozzarella cheese. Cover and cook over low heat for 15 minutes. Loosen the edges with a spatula and invert onto a serving platter.   *Serves 4.*

MELANZANE ALLA PARMIGIANA
EGGPLANT PARMESAN

Sometimes I will bake my eggplant instead of frying it to cut down on the amount of oil. Mammanon always fried hers. She used to lay the fried eggplant out on a layer of newspaper covered with a clean tablecloth. These days, paper towels will do.

3 medium-size eggplants

6 eggs, beaten

4 cups fine Italian bread crumbs, seasoned

Olive oil for frying

8 cups Marinara Sauce (see page 164)

2 cups grated Romano cheese

1 ½ pounds Mozzarella cheese, shredded

After you've washed the eggplants, slice them either lengthwise into chunky strips or into the more traditional round slices. Make the slices about 1/4 inch thick—not too thin or they will absorb too much oil. (Leave the skin on because the skin is where all the vitamins are. However, if the skin is too tough, you should peel it.) Place the eggplant slices in a colander or on layers of paper towels, sprinkle a little salt on the pieces, cover with another layer of paper towels, and hold it all down with something heavy like an iron. This will drain out the excess moisture, which is generally acidic. Drain for about 1 hour.

Dip each eggplant slice first in the beaten eggs, then coat it well in the bread crumbs. In a non-stick or cast-iron skillet, heat enough olive oil to fry the eggplant pieces. (I will sometimes bake the eggplant on a baking sheet.) Fry on

both sides until golden brown. Drain and cool the fried or baked eggplant slices on a layer of newspaper covered with paper towels. Preheat the oven to 350°F.

Spread enough Marinara Sauce on the bottom of the baking dish to coat it. Top with a layer of the eggplant slices. Cover with a layer of Mozzarella and Romano, then more of the sauce. Repeat, starting with a layer of the eggplant, until you fill the baking dish about 1/8 inch from the top. (Usually you can get 4 to 5 layers into a regular-size oblong glass baking dish.)

Bake for about 20 to 25 minutes, or until the Mozzarella cheese on top is melted. Let the dish settle for about 10 minutes before serving, so that when you're cutting the casserole into pieces it won't be too runny.   *Serves 6*.

POTATOES, PEPPERS, & EGGS

½ cup olive oil

4 large potatoes, diced

1 large green bell pepper, diced

1 large red bell pepper, diced

1 teaspoon salt

½ teaspoon pepper

1 tablespoon fresh oregano

¼ teaspoon fresh or dried chili
   peppers (optional)

8 large eggs

½ cup grated Romano cheese

1 cup diced Mozzarella cheese
   (optional)

When you make this dish, be sure to make extra. My kids loved it as a leftover—it was always one of their favorite things to put in a sandwich for lunch the next day.

In a large frying pan, heat the olive oil and brown the potatoes and peppers over low heat. Add the salt, pepper, oregano, and fresh or dried chilies if you've chosen the spicier version of this dish. Cook until the potatoes and peppers are tender and the potatoes are golden brown.

In a separate mixing bowl, whip the eggs with the grated cheese until frothy. Pour the mixture evenly over the vegetables. (If you want a cheesier dish, spread the Mozzarella cheese evenly over the eggs and vegetables.) Cook over low heat on one side.

As it cooks, gently loosen the edges. When all of the egg is cooked, turn it over and lightly brown. Serve immediately.
Serves 2 to 4.

POTATO & ONION OMELET

¼ cup olive oil

¼ cup butter

4 large potatoes, peeled and diced

1 large onion, diced

1 teaspoon salt

½ teaspoon pepper

1 teaspoon oregano

1 teaspoon chopped fresh or dried
   chili peppers

8 large eggs

½ cup grated cheese

Because this egg dish has fewer ingredients, I like to add some really hot chilis to give it a little zip. Be sure to use rubber gloves when you chop fresh hot chilis, though, or the "zip" will go into your fingers!

My daughter Annette on the stoop in New York.

In a large frying pan, heat the olive oil and butter. (In a non-stick or cast-iron frying pan, you could perhaps use half the oil and butter.) Also, depending on the size of your skillet, you may need to divide the ingredients in half and cook them in two batches. Add the potatoes and onion, and cook over low heat until they are tender and golden brown. As it cooks, add the salt, pepper, oregano, and chilies.

In a separate mixing bowl, whip the eggs with the grated cheese until the mixture is very frothy. (If you have an electric mixer, use it—it will save your arms!) Add the eggs to the potatoes and onions. Cook over low heat on one side. (As it cooks, gently loosen the edges of the omelet.) When all of the egg is cooked, turn the omelet over and brown the underside to a light golden color. Serve immediately. *Serves 4.*

EGGS FLORENTINE

2 tablespoons butter

2 tablespoons flour

1 cup milk (or half & half for a
   creamier sauce)

1 teaspoon Worcestershire sauce

1/4 teaspoon nutmeg

Salt and pepper to taste

2 cups cooked and chopped
   spinach

8 hardboiled eggs, thinly sliced

2 cups fine Italian bread crumbs,
   seasoned

1 cup freshly grated Romano
   cheese

1/4 cup chopped parsley

1/8 cup minced garlic

1/2 cup olive oil

1/2 teaspoon pepper

2 eggs

This dish is good for a late, leisurely breakfast—rare occasions around my house!—but we especially like it for a light dinner. I like to serve this dish with a warmed loaf of fresh Italian bread and a nice bottle of chilled white wine.

Melt the butter in a saucepan and stir in the flour over low heat. Slowly whisk in the milk or half & half, making sure the mixture doesn't lump or stick to the bottom of the pan as the mixture heats up and begins to bubble. Stir continuously. When the mixture begins to thicken, add the Worcestershire sauce, nutmeg, and salt and pepper to taste. Set aside.

Preheat the oven to 400°F.

Drain the spinach until most of the moisture is gone, and place in a lightly oiled glass baking dish. Cover with the slices of hardboiled eggs. In a bowl, combine the bread crumbs, grated cheese, chopped parsley, minced garlic, olive oil, pepper, and 2 raw eggs. This should be a coarsely textured mixture.

Sprinkle one half of the bread crumb mixture evenly over the eggs. Pour the white sauce evenly over the top of this, then cover with the rest of the bread crumb mixture. Cook in the oven until the topping is golden brown, about 15 minutes. Be sure not to burn! *Serves 4.*

ASPARAGUS OMELET

3 tablespoons olive oil

1 pound asparagus, cut into
   1-inch pieces

1 medium onion, chopped

1 cup chopped tomatoes

1 green bell pepper, chopped

1 teaspoon minced garlic

1/4 cup chopped fresh parsley

8 large eggs

1/2 teaspoon sweet basil

1/2 teaspoon oregano

1/2 cup grated Romano cheese

1/2 teaspoon salt

1/4 teaspoon pepper

This dish is delicious as a main meal, served with some leftover Potatoes Oreganata (see page 141), Roasted Peppers (see page 18), or Stuffed Mushrooms (see page 21).

Heat up the olive oil in a large skillet and add the asparagus, onion, tomatoes, green pepper, garlic, and parsley. Sauté over low heat until the asparagus are tender but still firm.

In a separate mixing bowl, whip the eggs with the remaining ingredients and pour over the vegetables in the skillet. Cook over very low heat until the

omelet starts to bubble. Then gently loosen the omelet around the edge of the skillet with a spatula. Continue to cook until it is done just about all the way through. Fold the omelet in half and cook for another minute or two, until lightly browned. *Serves 4.*

VARIATION

For a zucchini omelet, simply replace the asparagus with julienned zucchini.

VEGETABLES & SALADS

pulia, the region Poppanon and Mammanon came from, has been farming country for hundreds of years. And the dishes that Mammanon learned to cook when she was young are filled with the fresh vegetables that grew there. Like all Italian immigrants, the recipes she brought with her use vegetables in every imaginable way—baked, stuffed, roasted, sautéed, boiled, stewed, fried. And, of course, vegetables can be eaten raw in salads or cooked in sauces. In fact, if you look at the recipes in this book overall, you see that vegetables are more important in our family's way of eating than even meat, fish, or fowl.

It was from Mammanon and Poppanon that I learned to respect the importance of fresh, well-grown vegetables in good cooking. In Apulia, they were surrounded by a long tradition of talented Italian vegetable farmers, growers who really knew how to coax the best out of a vegetable. Italian farmers are well-known for their growing abilities—it isn't a mistake that here in America, we still use the Italian names for some of our vegetables: zucchini, broccoli, radicchio, to name a few.

Italian farmers had something in their favor: The south of Italy has a very long growing season, much like southern California—and even the north is temperate, with a longer growing season than most of the rest of Europe. This meant that Italian kitchens were filled with a steady stream of produce—and that vegetables were more affordable than meat or seafood. That is how vegetables became such an important part of Italian cooking.

But you must find the freshest vegetables possible, because your cooking can't be any better than the quality of your ingredients. That is why Mammanon and all the other ladies of her generation bought their vegetables fresh every day. (In fact, she bought extra vegetables and tomatoes when they were in season, and canned them so she could get the freshest possible taste after the growing season was over.) To this day I buy my vegetables every other day. How else can you have things as fresh as possible? Another thing: don't always go for the biggest. I learned from Mammanon that biggest is not always best. In fact, smaller vegetables—and fruits too—are usually juicier and have more flavor.

If you have good, fresh vegetables to start with, you can use the Italian approach to salads very effectively. And that approach is: keep it simple! Don't make a complicated dressing that calls attention to itself. Just coax out the natural flavors, aromas, textures, and colors of your ingredients.

Another trick that Mammanon taught me is: wash your vegetables in a bath of cold water and salt. This works particularly well for mushrooms and for leafy vegetables, which can be difficult to get completely clean. Swishing your vegetables in this cold salt-water bath takes every speck of dirt out, and leaves them very vigorous and fresh-looking.

Finally, if you want to make a good salad dressing, nothing is more important than the quality of your oil. And there really is only one kind of oil to use: extra virgin olive oil. There are many flavors of extra virgin olive oil. The flavor of the oil depends on all kinds of things—the country of origin, the kind of olives used, whether they were harvested early or late, what the weather was like during the growing season, and even who does the pressing. The lighter colored oils are drier, the darker ones are fruitier. You should experiment: find out what type of oil you like best. Remember, however, that your oil is one place you don't want to cut corners.

INSALATA DI SCAROLA
ESCAROLE SALAD

3 large cloves fresh garlic
½ cup olive oil
¼ cup red wine vinegar
½ teaspoon salt
½ teaspoon pepper
1 bunch escarole
1 bunch romaine lettuce
1 large cucumber
1 large red onion
½ dozen mushrooms
½ dozen radishes
¼ cup capers
Coarsely grated Romano cheese

Escarole Salad and Escarole Soup (see page 35) were always staples in Mammanon's cooking. She used to grow it in her small vegetable garden behind her deli. It used to be harder to find in American markets, but these days you'll find it easy to enjoy this classic Italian country taste.

Put the garlic cloves through a garlic press and mix with the olive oil, wine vinegar, salt, and pepper. With a rubber spatula, spread this mixture evenly over the bottom of a large wooden salad bowl.

Wash the escarole and romaine well and tear into bite-size pieces in the wooden bowl. Wash, peel, and thinly slice the cucumber and the red onion, and add them to the lettuce. Wash the mushrooms and radishes well in a cold salt-water bath. Remove their stems, slice them thinly, and add them to the salad bowl.

Add the capers, and toss the salad well, coating it with the dressing. You may wish to adjust the seasonings to suit your taste. Sprinkle each serving with some Romano cheese.   *Serves 4 to 6.*

INSALATA RUSTICA
PEASANT SALAD

2 pounds red potatoes
½ pound bacon
1 head escarole
1 head romaine lettuce
2 large red onions, sliced into thin
  rings
¼ pound salami, thinly sliced
¾ cup olive oil
Juice of 2 lemons
3 tablespoons dry white wine
2 cloves garlic
1 tablespoon brown mustard
½ teaspoon salt
¼ teaspoon pepper

This is a hearty salad. It's made with an unusual combination of fresh ingredients that are very filling—it could almost be a meal in itself!

In a large pot, cover the potatoes with cold water and bring to a boil. Reduce the heat and cook until they are tender when poked with a fork. Drain, and let cool long enough to handle. Slice into thin slices, and set aside to cool completely.

Fry the bacon in a skillet over low heat until crispy, about 10 to 15 minutes. Transfer to paper towels to drain, then cut into strips and set aside.

Wash the salad greens in a bath of cold, salted water. Drain, and dry on paper towels. Tear into small, bite-size pieces and place in a very large salad bowl. Add the potato slices, onions, salami, and bacon pieces.

Combine the olive oil, lemon juice, wine, garlic, mustard, salt, and pepper in a blender, and blend until smooth. Pour over the salad and toss well. Adjust the salt and pepper to taste.

Serves 6.

There's Poppanon and Mammanon with my daugher Annette on Annette's birthday.

STUFFED EGGPLANT FROM FOGGIA

4 small eggplants, halved lengthwise

¼ cup fresh parsley

2 heaping tablespoons capers

½ cup sliced black olives

1 teaspoon salt

½ teaspoon pepper

1 tablespoon chopped fresh basil

¼ cup + 2 tablespoons olive oil

1 large onion, chopped

1 cup chopped tomatoes

3 cloves garlic, minced

2 cups Ricotta cheese

½ cup Italian bread crumbs, seasoned

½ cup grated Romano cheese

½ teaspoon oregano

Mammanon brought this dish with her from where she grew up in Italy. She just called it stuffed eggplant, but I call it "di Foggia" to remember where she came from, and everything she gave me from there.

Scoop out the eggplant pulp, cut into 1/2-inch cubes, and place in a large mixing bowl. Mix in the parsley, capers, olives, salt, pepper, and basil. Reserve the eggplant shells.

Preheat the oven to 350°F. Heat 1/4 cup of the olive oil in a skillet. Sauté the onion, tomatoes, and garlic over low heat. Do not brown. Pour this mixture into the diced eggplant mixture and stir well. Fold in the Ricotta cheese, then fill the eggplant shells with this mixture and set in a well-oiled baking dish or casserole.

In a small mixing bowl, combine the bread crumbs, grated cheese, and oregano with the remaining olive oil. Sprinkle over the top of the eggplant halves, covering each one well. Cover the casserole and bake for 45 minutes. Remove the cover and bake for another 15 minutes.
Serves 4 to 6.

ARTICHOKE & CHESTNUT SALAD

2 dozen whole, unpeeled chestnuts

1 cup olive oil

2 large leeks, thinly sliced

¼ cup minced garlic

1 ½ cups artichoke hearts,
   rinsed and drained

¼ cup fresh lemon juice

¼ cup dry white wine

1 teaspoon sugar

1 teaspoon basil

Salt and pepper to taste

1 head romaine lettuce, washed
   and drained

½ cup coarsely grated Romano
   cheese

½ cup pine nuts

This is a salad that you can impress your friends with. It is very unusual and elegant—but most of all, it is delicious!

Boil the chestnuts in a large pot of salted water until tender. Drain and let cool.

Peel off the shells and slice the chestnuts into thin slices. You can also use canned chestnuts, but be sure to rinse them well before you slice them. Set aside.

Heat the olive oil in a large skillet and add the leeks and garlic. Sauté for 2 or 3 minutes, being careful not to brown.

Slice the artichoke hearts and add them and the chestnuts to the skillet. Sauté for another 2 or 3 minutes, then add the lemon juice, wine, sugar, and basil. Simmer for 5 minutes, then remove from the heat. While cooling, season with salt and pepper.

Tear the lettuce into bite-size pieces and place in a large salad bowl. Toss in the cooled chestnut mixture, along with the grated cheese and the pine nuts. *Serves 4.*

PISELLI AL PROSCIUTTO
PEAS WITH PROSCIUTTO

1 tablespoon olive oil
1 large onion, diced
3 cloves garlic, minced
1 tablespoon butter
½ pound prosciutto, cut into
   small strips
1 tablespoon brown sugar
1 pound snow peas (steamed and
   drained)
Salt and pepper (optional)

This vegetable dish goes well with just about any main course. I like to serve it with roasted or broiled fish. If you can't find snow peas, frozen green peas work just as well.

Heat the olive oil in a large skillet and add the onion and garlic. Sauté over medium heat until the onions are clear. Do not brown.

Add the butter and the prosciutto, then stir in the brown sugar. Sauté for just a minute or two, then add the snow peas and toss. Some people add just a pinch of salt and pepper before serving, but I think the dish is delicious without it.

Serves 4.

INSALATA DI CANNELLINI AL TONNO
CANNELLINI BEAN & TUNA SALAD

2 cups cannellini (white kidney) beans
1 pound fresh tuna
2 red bell peppers, diced
1 large red onion, diced
2 tablespoons chopped fresh parsley
2 tablespoons lemon juice
3 large cloves garlic
½ cup olive oil
Salt and pepper to taste
1 head radicchio or escarole

Tuna salad is an American favorite— so why not try it made the Italian way?

Soak the beans overnight. Rinse, cover with water in a large pot, and boil over medium heat until tender. Rinse again, and set aside in a large mixing bowl to cool. (If you use canned beans, be sure to rinse them well.)

Place the tuna in a skillet with about 1/2 cup of water. Poach the tuna, covered, over medium heat until tender and flaky,

about 10 minutes. Remove the fish from the water and transfer it to a plate to cool.

Using a fork, flake the tuna into bite-size flakes, and add them to the beans. Add the red peppers, onion, and parsley, and toss lightly. Blend the lemon juice, garlic, and olive oil in a blender. Pour over the salad and toss gently. Season with salt and pepper. Serve on a bed of radicchio or escarole.

Serves 4.

My daughter Marilyn after her senior prom.

TOMATO SALAD NEAPOLITAN STYLE

8 large tomatoes

2 red onions

2 yellow onions

2 cucumbers

1 cup olive oil

¼ cup red wine vinegar

1 teaspoon sugar

1 tablespoon minced garlic

2 teaspoons chopped fresh oregano

Salt and pepper to taste

1 head romaine lettuce

Hardboiled egg slices

This salad is a good way to show off really good, fresh tomatoes. You may want to make it in the summer months when you can find the most beautiful variety of tasty, ripe tomatoes at your market.

Cut the tomatoes and onions into small wedges. Take the onion layers apart. Peel the cucumbers, dice, and add to the mixture. Toss the vegetables together in a large mixing bowl.

Add the olive oil, wine vinegar, sugar, garlic, oregano, salt, and pepper, and toss together well. Marinate in the refrigerator overnight.

Wash the lettuce in a cold, salt-water bath, drain, and tear into bite-size pieces. Serve the marinated tomato salad over beds of lettuce, garnished with slices of hardboiled eggs.

Serves 4 to 6.

POTATOES OREGANATA

8 large red or white potatoes

2 onions

³/₄ cup olive oil

¹/₄ cup water

¹/₄ cup garlic, minced

¹/₂ cup chopped parsley

1 heaping tablespoon chopped fresh oregano

1 ¹/₂ cups fine Italian bread crumbs, seasoned

2 eggs

1 cup grated Romano cheese

Salt and pepper to taste

In my family, a popular Sunday dinner main course is a big stuffed and roasted chicken surrounded by these potatoes. And I tell you, the leftovers make a delicious lunch the next day, too. In my busy household, that is always something to look forward to!

Preheat the oven to 350°F.

Wash the potatoes well, leaving their skins on. Slice the potatoes into small, thin wedges lengthwise, and the onions into thin arcs.

Place the potatoes and onions in a large mixing bowl and coat them with 1/2 cup olive oil. Sprinkle the water over them and bake in a large glass baking dish until they are slightly tender but still firm, about 30 minutes.

In a small mixing bowl, combine the garlic, parsley, oregano, bread crumbs, eggs, the other 1/4 cup of olive oil, and grated cheese. The mixture should have a coarse consistency. Remove the baking dish from the oven and evenly cover the potatoes and onions with the bread crumb mixture. (You may need to add more bread crumbs so that all the moisture from the potatoes and onions is absorbed into the bread crumb mixture.)

Bake until the topping is golden and the potatoes are completely tender, approximately 20 minutes.   *Serves 4 to 6.*

SEAFOOD SALAD

This is a dish we almost always start with as an antipasto or appetizer for our traditional Christmas Eve seafood feast. In the summer months, if I want something light and healthy, I will very often serve it as a main course. The two secrets to its mouth-watering flavor are to use the absolute freshest seafood ingredients and to cut everything into uniform pieces so that the combination of all the ingredients is tasted in each bite.

1 pound shrimp, peeled and deveined

1 pound baby clams, shelled

2 pounds mussels, shelled

$\frac{1}{2}$ pound scallops

$\frac{1}{2}$ pound scungilli (conch meat), cut
    into chunks

$\frac{1}{2}$ pound calamari, cut into rings

$\frac{1}{2}$ pound octopus, cut into chunks (optional)

3 stalks celery, cut into small cubes

2 red bell peppers, cut into small cubes

$\frac{1}{2}$ cup pitted green olives, cut in halves

$\frac{1}{2}$ cup pitted sweet black olives, cut
    in halves

$\frac{1}{2}$ cup pitted Italian black olives, cut
    in halves

$\frac{1}{8}$ cup minced garlic

1 teaspoon oregano

1 cup olive oil

$\frac{1}{2}$ cup red wine vinegar

1 teaspoon chopped fresh mint

$\frac{1}{4}$ cup chopped fresh parsley

Salt and pepper to taste

Wash all the shrimp, clams, mussels, scallops, scungilli, calamari, and octopus (if you use it) in cold, salted water, and steam for about 10 minutes. (If you prefer your clams and shrimp raw, it is an option to have some of the seafood raw and some steamed in the same salad.) Be sure not to steam the fish for too long or it will be tough, and you want all the fish to be fresh and tender. Drain the fish well and pat dry.

In a large mixing bowl, combine the seafood with the remaining ingredients, and marinate for at least an hour before serving. Garnish with extra sprigs of fresh parsley and mint.   *Serves 8.*

NOTES

1. If you are serving this seafood salad as an appetizer, include a variety of olives, a nice fresh loaf of Italian bread, and perhaps the Vegetables Oreganata (see page 146).

2. Scungilli is the delicate and delicious meat from the inside of the conch shell. For some, it may be hard to find.

That's Atlantic City in 1953 again. My son Neil is with his friends, Fat Ralphie, Johny Twin, Franky Gioa, and Louie Black.

BELL PEPPER SALAD

"Peppers go with fish," my mother used to tell me. This salad is delicious with most seafood dishes.

3 large red peppers, sliced in thin rings
3 large green peppers, sliced in thin rings
2 large leeks, sliced in thin rings
1 tablespoon minced garlic
$1/8$ cup red wine vinegar

$1/2$ cup olive oil
$1/4$ cup chopped fresh mint
1 tablespoon chopped fresh oregano
$1/4$ cup chopped fresh parsley
Salt and pepper to taste
1 teaspoon minced red, green, or yellow hot
   peppers (optional)
3 heads Belgian endive

In a large salad bowl, combine the red and green peppers, leeks, garlic, olive oil, red wine vinegar, mint, oregano, and parsley. Toss gently and season with salt and pepper.

For a hot and spicy salad, add the minced hot peppers and toss into the salad. Let marinate for at least 1 hour before serving. Serve the salad over leaves of Belgian endive.
Serves 4.

POTATO PIE

It's best to use red potatoes in this recipe. Be sure to leave the peels on them because that's where all your vitamins are, and potatoes are full of them. The peels also keep the delicious potato flavors inside the potato!

CRUST
1 $1/2$ cups all-purpose flour
$1/2$ teaspoon salt
$1/4$ cup butter
3 tablespoons water

In a large bowl, sift together the flour and salt. Work the butter into the flour mixture with a pastry cutter or your fingertips until the flour mixture is mealy. Add the water, mix, and form into a ball. Refrigerate for 20 to 30 minutes. Roll out the dough and then press into a large pie dish. Set aside.

POTATO LAYER
6 cups potatoes, cubed
1 cup half & half
$1/2$ cup olive oil
2 tablespoons butter
Salt and pepper to taste

Cover the potatoes with water in a large pot. Boil them until they are tender, then drain. In a large mixing bowl, use an electric mixer to whip the potatoes with the half & half, olive oil, and butter. Season with salt and pepper to taste, and set aside.

TOMATO LAYER
6 cups tomatoes, chopped
2 $1/2$ cups diced Mozzarella cheese
1 tablespoon oregano
2 tablespoons minced garlic
1 teaspoon salt
$1/2$ teaspoon pepper

In a mixing bowl, stir all of the ingredients together.

BREAD CRUMB LAYER
4 cups fine Italian bread crumbs, seasoned
1 cup olive oil
1 cup coarsely grated Romano or Parmesan cheese
$1/8$ cup minced garlic
$1/2$ cup minced parsley
2 eggs

In a mixing bowl, combine all of the ingredients into a coarse consistency, and set aside. Preheat the oven to 375°F.

ASSEMBLY

Spread one half of the whipped potato mixture over the pie crust. Cover with one half of the tomato mixture, then with one half of the bread crumb mixture. Repeat the layering, then bake until the pie crust and the bread crumb topping are golden brown, about 30 minutes. Slice and serve hot. *Serves 4 to 6.*

CAULIFLOWER WITH BACON

1 large head cauliflower
$1/2$ pound bacon
3 tablespoons olive oil
1 large onion, minced
2 large cloves garlic, minced
2 cups chopped tomatoes
2 cups chicken broth
1 cup grated Romano cheese
Salt and pepper to taste
Parsley sprigs for garnish

This tasty vegetable dish can be served as a side dish when you present your main course—or right afterward.

Wash the cauliflower and separate into florets. Place in a pot of boiling water and cook until tender. Drain, and set aside.

In a skillet, cook the bacon to a golden brown. Set aside to drain on paper towels.

Heat the olive oil in a skillet, and sauté the onion and garlic until the onion is clear. Add the tomatoes and the broth, and let simmer for 10 minutes. Chop the bacon into small pieces and add to the skillet.

Place the cauliflower pieces in a large mixing bowl, and fold in the sauce, then the grated cheese. Season with salt and pepper. Serve on a warmed platter garnished with some sprigs of fresh parsley. *Serves 4 to 6.*

VEGETABLES OREGANATA

1 pound asparagus, trimmed

1 large eggplant

4 large zucchini

2 ½ cups fine Italian bread crumbs, seasoned

½ cup olive oil

1 tablespoon oregano

¼ cup chopped fresh parsley

1 tablespoon minced garlic

¾ cup grated Romano cheese

½ teaspoon salt

¼ teaspoon pepper

2 eggs

½ pound shredded Mozzarella cheese (optional)

Try using the vegetables that I suggest in this dish. These are traditional, and they are delicious prepared this way. But always use the vegetables that are in season and that look the freshest at your local market—they'll work the best.

Wash and cut all of the vegetables into 3-inch spears. Don't peel the eggplant or zucchini—they are tastier with their peels left on. Bring a large pot of water to a boil, drop in all the vegetable spears, and parboil them until they are tender but still firm, about 1 1/2 to 2 minutes. Drain on paper towels and let cool.

Preheat the broiler. In a mixing bowl, combine the bread crumbs, 1/2 cup of the olive oil, the oregano, parsley, garlic, grated cheese, eggs, salt, and pepper. The mixture should have a coarse consistency.

Lay the vegetables out in an oiled baking dish, alternating them. Spread the bread-crumb mixture over them evenly. Sprinkle them lightly with the shredded Mozzarella cheese, if desired. Broil them in the oven just long enough for the bread crumb mixture to lightly brown, and for the cheese to melt. Serve immediately. (If the vegetables have cooled down prior to serving, pop them in the broiler to heat and crisp up—but be sure not to brown the Mozzarella cheese.)

Serves 4 to 6.

NOTE: Red bell peppers and carrots can be added to the vegetables for more color.

WHITE BEANS NEAPOLITAN STYLE

4 cups cannellini (white kidney)
   beans, soaked overnight
½ cup olive oil
2 large stalks leeks, chopped
1 tablespoon minced garlic
2 cups chopped tomatoes
½ cup chopped fresh parsley
2 tablespoons chopped fresh basil
1 teaspoon salt
½ teaspoon pepper

My daughter-in-law is a vegetarian, and this is one of her favorite dishes. But whether or not you are a vegetarian, try serving it along with some fluffy rice, and I'm sure everyone will love it.

Wash the beans, cover with water in a large pot, and bring to a boil. Simmer until tender. You may have to add more water half-way through the cooking. Remove from the heat, rinse, and drain.

Heat the olive oil in a large skillet. Sauté the leeks and garlic until tender. Add the tomatoes, parsley, basil, salt, pepper, and the beans, and stir well. Cover, and simmer for about 20 minutes. Adjust the seasoning to taste. *Serves 4.*

In old Italy, they call the secret ingredient "The hand of the cook." It's the hand of the cook that expresses the heart.

SUNDAY DINNER

HEN WE WERE WORKING ON THIS BOOK, MY SON NEIL AND I GOT TO TALKING ABOUT THE SUNDAY DINNERS OUR FAMILY HAS EACH WEEK—for Italian Americans, every Sunday is a big feast day. I loved one of his stories so much, I thought he should tell it to you:

"When we were kids growing up in Little Italy, no matter how far from home our play on Sunday afternoon took us, we made it home in time for dinner. Those Sunday dinners were the core of our family life. Not only that, the food was fantastic. As kids, and later as adults, we cherished the event for both reasons.

But one Sunday dinner I'll never forget. That was the day my wife, who was not Italian, got her first big test in Italian cooking. I was the first one in the family to marry an American—that is, an American who was not Italian.

When we got married, I was just out of the service. I was in a hurry and I didn't follow the tradition in my family for such things. My wife and I went to a wedding chapel in Las Vegas and got married there by a justice of the peace. No one from the family was there, so my grandfather, Poppanon, the patriarch of the family had serious reservations about my marriage. In fact, for quite some time afterwards, he didn't speak to me. Then, one day, Mammanon called me. She spoke only broken English, but she told me, in essence, "I've been talking to Poppanon about you. He's getting better now about your marriage. You have to be patient with him. He's so old-fashioned, you know."

I knew it couldn't have been any easier for her—she was from the Old Country, too. And she liked to hang on to the old customs just as much as he did. But she really wanted to see peace in the family. So, finally, she told me, "Come on over."

"It's alright with Poppanon?" I asked.

"Si. He wants to talk to you. I think everything will be alright."

I rushed right over. Mammanon was at the stove, like always, and Poppanon was sitting at the kitchen table, where we had had so many family feasts together. He was slicing peaches and dunking them into his glass of homemade wine. First thing, he asked me, "Did you eat?"

"Yes. I just finished having lunch." He brushed my response aside.

"Your grandmother will make you something to eat. Christina, make him something to eat." He was definitely in charge of this conversation, and I was going to eat some of Mammanon's food!

"You want some wine?" He asked me next. I knew it was his own homemade wine, and I knew by now what I had better say. "Yes, sure. Thanks." I could see we weren't going to be able to talk until I had some food, so I started slicing peaches along with Poppanon and dunking them in the glass of rich red wine he had poured me. I was enjoying the whole situation immensely. I loved both Poppanon and Mammanon and I knew it would work out somehow, but the situation was so dramatic, just like a scene from one of the classic Italian operettas Poppanon had taken me to.

When Mammanon put a plate of food, delicious-smelling as always, on the table in front of me, Poppanon was ready to get down to business.

"You got married?" He asked in his half-Italian, half-English.

I answered "Yes." And even though I played it very seriously, I was bursting with laughter inside. As if he didn't know already!

"Where'd you get married?"

"I got married in Las Vegas."

"You get married in a church in Las Vegas?"

"Well, it was like a church."

"What do you mean, like a church? It's either a church or it's not a church! Did you get married in a church, or no?"

"It was a chapel."

"A chapel is not a church."

"Alright, it wasn't a church."

It was really quiet. This was definitely the Old World facing the New. I had made a real break with the family tradition by not having a big fancy wedding in a church. And my grandfather had worked very hard to keep his family together, by upholding customs just like this one from the Old Country. He cut a couple more slices of peach, and took a few more sips of wine.

"Who'd you marry?" he asked, as if all of this was news to him, and he hadn't heard it a million times already from the rest of my relatives. Finally, it came out. My wife was American.

"Amerigon!?" he asked, in his Italian accent.

"Yes, Poppanon. She's American." More quiet. Another bite of peach, another sip of wine.

"Why'd you get married?"

"Because I love her." Now we were getting down to it! Poppanon finally burst out with what seemed to be his real concern about my marriage.

"Love! Lova nonsense! Howa you gonna eat? She doesn't know how to make Italian food! You gonna starve to death!"

By now, I couldn't contain it any more. I burst out laughing. Mammanon was giggling, too. Of course, Poppanon gave her a dirty look for that, and then he turned to me and gave me a dirty look, too. We had to keep quiet and take this seriously. So we bit our lips and waited to hear what he had to say next.

There was another long pause, very dramatic. And, of course, more wine, more peaches. Finally, he gave his directive.

"You better have your mother and your grandmother teach this girl how to cook."

I was forgiven. Poppanon now felt that the family would be preserved! But there were terms. I knew my wife would be game, so I agreed. She started cooking with Elodia and Mammanon, learning the Italian immigrant cooking in this cookbook. Finally, a few months later, my wife and I invited Poppanon over to our house for Sunday dinner.

You can see a lot of the family in this photo. From the left, that's my sister-in-law Anna with her son Rocky, my brother Jimmy, Mammanon, and Poppanon with my brother Tony standing behind him and my daughter Annette in front. Then, there's Tony's wife Lucy, my son Neil, me, and my husband Gaetano. We all got together to celebrate Mammanon and Poppanon's silver anniversary in 1949.

who were trying to look serious, while suppressing our amusement! Finally, Poppanon made his pronouncement, "Bon. Bon." It was good—cheers went up around the table, and out in the kitchen! He enjoyed the whole meal, he and my wife became great friends. Poppanon was satisfied that the family was intact and that I would eat well. With my mother Elodia and my grandmother Mammanon as her principal teachers, my wife mastered our style of Italian immigrant cooking.

Later, when my wife and I moved to southern

Since Sunday dinner traditionally starts at three in the afternoon, Elodia, Mammanon, and a whole bunch of my aunts and cousins collected in our kitchen with my wife—starting at about eight in the morning. They talked and laughed and cooked all day. I think half of the best Italian cooks in Brooklyn were in our apartment that day. They turned out a fantastic feast—a real classic Italian Sunday spread with antipasti of every kind, soup, a big pasta dish—manicotti, meat dishes—a couple of roasted chickens, a lemon chicken, pork, all kinds of vegetable dishes on the side and beautiful salads. There was so much food!

When my grandfather finally arrived in the afternoon, they were ready—and nervous, like it was the President of the United States they had cooked dinner for! Poppanon walked into our apartment, and first thing, he kissed our new baby. Then we all sat down to eat. As the meal began, I could tell that the antipasti and the soup were pleasing to him. But the real test was yet to come—the pasta dish. When the manicotti was served, the ladies were all on the edges of their chairs, leaning forward, watching Poppanon put that first bite to his mouth. You could hear a pin drop.

He chewed it slowly, savoring it, making his decision about whether an "Amerigon" girl could cook Italian food the right way or not. I don't think anyone breathed—except for my father and I,

California, we found nothing that resembled those great Sunday dinners in Little Italy in Brooklyn. When I would describe them to my new friends on the West Coast, I could tell that my friends thought I was exaggerating—that is, until we began to invite them to our house for Sunday dinners done in Italian immigrant style. Soon, I noticed that I was hearing all kinds of hints, angling for an invitation to one of our West Coast Sunday feasts!

Whenever I am in New York and invite anyone to Sunday dinner at Elodia's apartment, I prepare them to enjoy themselves. I tell them stories about our Sunday dinner tradition, and I describe the food so that they will be looking forward to a truly great meal. But no matter how much I build it up in advance, my friends are always amazed at how delicious and bountiful Elodia's meals are.

Even though the food is plentiful beyond compare, after Sunday dinner is over and you reflect back on it, you realize that more time was spent enjoying the company of your family and friends than was spent eating. When I was a kid, I thought it was mainly about the food. But now I know that for my grandmother, Mammanon, and for my mother, Elodia, who spent so many hours preparing those Sunday meals, being with family and friends is the real point. Our fabulous Sunday meals are really a platform to strengthen the bonds between family members and friends, and to create a way for the warmth of this cultural heritage to be shared.

ORANGE SALAD

8 sweet oranges, peeled and
  chilled
¼ cup olive oil
¼ cup chopped fresh mint
Salt and pepper to taste
Fresh arugula or romaine lettuce

This is the simplest salad to make, but refreshing and delicious. On a hot summer day, my kids love to make a meal of it. Be sure to chill your oranges well, because the cooler the salad the more delicious. When I make it for my friends, I serve it on a bed of arugula, along with a loaf of Italian bread, a plate of assorted cheeses, and a chilled white wine. I guarantee that after you make it the first time, you will always double and triple the recipe from then on.

Cut the oranges into bite-size pieces and place in a mixing bowl. Toss with the olive oil, fresh mint, and salt and pepper. Serve over fresh greens.   *Serves 4.*

VARIATION
When in season, this dish is delicious with the oranges combined with pieces of watermelon. (Be sure to remove the seeds from the watermelon.)

INSALATA CAMPESTRE

ARUGULA & DANDELION SALAD

1 pound cannellini (white kidney)
  beans, soaked overnight
4 large cloves fresh garlic
1 cup olive oil
¼ cup chopped fresh basil
1 teaspoon salt
½ teaspoon pepper
1 teaspoon sugar
½ cup red wine vinegar
½ bunch arugula
½ bunch fresh dandelions
½ bunch romaine lettuce

You may not be able to get dandelions from your corner produce stand— even in my neighborhood, they are getting harder and harder to get ahold of. If you've never tried them, I would really try to find some. They're sweet, and with a little olive oil, garlic, and seasoning, they're absolutely wonderful. Sometimes I'll add other vegetables to this salad as well. Some of my favorites are red onions, tomatoes, and some grated yellow squash.

In a large pot, cover the cannellini beans with water and bring to a boil. Simmer until tender. Drain well, rinse, then drain again. Let cool.

Place the garlic, olive oil, basil, salt, pepper, sugar, and red wine vinegar in a blender and blend well.

Wash the arugula, fresh dandelions, and romaine lettuces well in a cold, salt-water bath. Drain, and tear into bite-size pieces. Place in a large wooden salad bowl, and blend the different types of lettuces together. Add the cannellini beans. Pour the dressing over the salad and toss well. At this time you can add any other type of vegetable you might like, and toss well with the salad.   *Serves 4 to 6.*

The way we cook, things like garlic, basil, and vinegar are not just for taste. They keep you healthy.

ELODIA'S ITALIAN POTATO SALAD

If you want something different on a summer picnic, try potato salad the Italian way!

8 large red potatoes
1 pound string beans
3 large ripe tomatoes, chopped
1 large red onion, chopped
3 to 4 stalks celery, chopped
1 cucumber, peeled and chopped
1/4 cup coarsely chopped fresh parsley
1/8 cup coarsely chopped fresh mint
1 cup pitted black olives, whole or sliced
1 cup olive oil
1/2 cup balsamic or red wine vinegar

1/2 tablespoon minced fresh oregano
1 tablespoon minced garlic
2 tablespoons brown mustard
2 egg yolks
Salt and pepper to taste
Slices of hardboiled egg
Sprigs of parsley and mint

Bring a large pot of water to a boil. Boil the potatoes until tender. Drain, and let cool slightly, then cut into small cubes.

While the potatoes are cooking, steam the string beans until tender but still firm. Cut them into 1/2-inch pieces and place in a large mixing bowl.

Add the potatoes, tomatoes, onion, celery, cucumber, parsley, mint, and olives.

Blend the olive oil, vinegar, oregano, garlic, mustard, and egg yolks in a blender and fold into the salad. Season with salt and pepper, then chill in the refrigerator for at least an hour before serving. (The next day it's always better!) Garnish with slices of hardboiled egg and sprigs of parsley and mint.

Serves 4 to 6.

ITALIAN PASTA & BEAN SALAD

1 pound rotini (spiral) pasta
2 cups precooked garbanzo ("ceci") beans, drained and cooled
2 cups chopped fresh tomatoes
3/4 cup diced red onions
3/4 cup sliced Italian green olives
3/4 cup sliced black olives
1/2 cup chopped fresh parsley
3/4 cup extra virgin olive oil
2 tablespoons red wine or balsamic vinegar
2 egg yolks
1/8 cup minced garlic
1 teaspoon Worcestershire sauce
1 tablespoon dry mustard
Salt and pepper to taste
1 teaspoon sugar (optional)

It might be more convenient for you to use canned garbanzo beans in this dish than to cook them from scratch. Of course, if you take the time to cook them, you will find that they have a lot more flavor and taste fresher. (If you use the canned beans, be sure to rinse them thoroughly with cold water, and you may need to add just a bit more spices.)

Bring a large pot of water to a boil and cook the pasta al dente (still somewhat firm). Rinse, drain, and cool.

In a large mixing bowl, stir the cooled garbanzo beans into the pasta. Add the tomatoes, red onions, parsley, and olives.

Blend the olive oil, vinegar, egg yolks, garlic, Worcestershire sauce, mustard, salt, pepper, and sugar in a blender and toss into the salad. Chill for at least an hour before serving (overnight is better).

Serves 4.

VARIATION
You can substitute cannellini beans for the garbanzo beans, or you can use half of each.

That's me (in the center) with my son Neil (on the right) and some friends at a party at my home in Brooklyn. It's 1954.

MARINATED VEGETABLES

1/2 pound mushrooms, stems removed
1 large cauliflower, broken into florets
2 green bell peppers, cut into
   1/2-inch strips
2 large red onions, cut into chunks
1 cup olive oil
2 tablespoons minced garlic
1/2 cup red wine vinegar
1 tablespoon sugar
1 teaspoon salt
1/2 teaspoon pepper

What can I say? This dish is an Italian classic. It goes with everything!

Steam the vegetables until tender but still firm and slightly crunchy, and place in a large bowl. Add the olive oil, garlic, vinegar, sugar, salt, and pepper, and toss well. Let marinate for at least an hour (overnight is better).

Serve the vegetables on an antipasto plate with cheeses and meats, or along with a nice green leafy salad, or you could even toss some cooked pasta, preferably spirals, into the vegetables for a cool pasta salad in the summer months. If you want it to be spicier, add some crushed hot red peppers to the marinade. *Serves 4.*

ITALIAN TEMPURA

This recipe was one of my father's favorites, and it is mine, too. My mother would prepare it with a wide variety of vegetables. I've made it with different kinds of fish, parboiled sweetbreads, chicken, and veal. Like much of my family's cooking, one recipe—done with different ingredients—makes many dishes!

2 cups all-purpose flour
1 teaspoon salt
1/2 teaspoon pepper
1/3 cup olive oil
1 1/2 cups warm water
An assortment of vegetables*

Salt and pepper to taste
3 egg whites, beaten until stiff
Olive oil for deep frying
Fresh parsley, finely chopped
Thin slices of lemon

* A combination of the following cut into strips: carrots, green beans, eggplant (unpeeled), green, red, or yellow bell peppers, zucchini; yellow onion, cut into wedges; cauliflower and broccoli, broken into florets; artichoke hearts, cut in half; mushroom caps; firm tomatoes, cut into wedges.

Sift the flour, salt, and pepper into a bowl. Stir in the olive oil, then slowly beat in the warm water. The consistency should be creamy and thick. Place all of the vegetables on a tray, and sprinkle them liberally with salt and pepper. Fold the stiff egg whites into the batter mixture.

Heat some oil in a deep skillet, then dip several pieces at a time of the vegetables into the batter and fry to a golden brown. Drain on paper towels, then transfer to the oven to keep warm. Serve sprinkled with the parsley and surrounded with lemon slices.

VARIATION
Try serving this dish drizzled with a thick Marinara Sauce (see page 164) and sprinkled with grated Parmesan or Romano cheese.

CARAMELIZED CARROTS IN MARSALA

1/2 cup butter
2 pounds carrots, julienned
2 tablespoons brown sugar
1 cup Marsala wine
Salt and pepper to taste

This dish goes with just about any of our meat dishes, or you can enjoy it all by itself. And it is so delicious that no one will believe how fast and easy it is to prepare!

Melt the butter in a deep skillet. Add the carrots and sauté over medium heat, about 5 minutes. Be sure not to brown the carrots.

Sprinkle the carrots with the brown sugar, stir, then add the Marsala. Cover, and simmer until the carrots are tender but still firm.

Remove the cover and continue to simmer. The liquid should be evaporating and the sauce in the carrots should begin to brown and caramelize. Season with salt and pepper. *Serves 4.*

SALSE E CONDIMENTI
SAUCES

What do you think of when you think of great sauce-making? Do you think of French cooking, like most people? Maybe, like me, you didn't know that the art of making sauces was actually born in Italy. My son Neil, who grew up on home-made Italian sauces, tells me that the French learned about making sauces from the Italians, from the cooks that Catherine de Medici brought with her when she left Italy and traveled to France, all the way back in 1533.

It makes sense that sauce-making started in Italy, because in Italian cooking, nothing is more important than the sauce. Every good Italian cook can make delicious sauces—in Italy, how can you call yourself a cook if you can't make a sauce? The sauce is the soul of our cooking. It is the sauce that defines the dish. The Italian approach to making sauces (and to cooking in general) is simple: use fresh, quality ingredients and cook them slowly to bring out their natural flavors. If you were to order the same sauce in a dozen restaurants in different parts of Italy, you would get a dozen different sauces—depending on the region, on what is fresh and in season, on the family tradition of the cook, and so on. There is no such thing as one precise way to make any Italian sauce.

Now that we are talking about Italian sauces, you are probably thinking, "tomatoes." But not every Italian sauce is made from tomatoes. Overall, Italian sauces are usually based on olive oil, wine, garlic, and herbs. Bread, cheese, and a variety of vegetables can also be added, to give body to the sauce. (And, as far as vegetables go, corn, carrots, and peppers are just as common in my cooking as tomatoes.) That is not to say that Italy doesn't deserve its fame for tomato sauce. When tomatoes were introduced to Italy many years ago, the tomatoes were small, knobby, and unappetizing. It was the genius of Italian farmers—who have always raised the most tasty varieties of fruits and vegetables—that transformed those early tomatoes into large, juicy varieties that could be made into so many delicious sauces. So, as Italians, we are proud of our tomatoes—they were one of our earliest exports to the new world. I have even heard that Thomas Jefferson was one of the first Americans to import Italian tomato seeds to the United States!

One last thing: Everyone thinks it takes a long time to make a good fresh pasta sauce from scratch. It's really not true. My daughter-in-law said she had always used bottled sauces before she married my son, because she has a career and didn't have time to make sauce at home. But the sauces I learned about from Mammanon are easy to make, and you can make some of them in 20 to 30 minutes! After I taught her to make Mammanon's good, quick marinara sauce, she couldn't believe it! She has told me that she never used bottled sauce again—the fresh sauce is just too good and too easy to make!

All Italians know that "hunger is the best sauce."

BROOKLYN MEAT "GRAVY"

2 tablespoons olive oil

1 ½ cups chopped onion

¼ cup minced garlic

5 pounds tomatoes

1 tablespoon oregano

1 tablespoon basil

Salt and pepper to taste

1 tablespoon sugar

2 pounds Italian sausages
   (some sweet, some spicy)

Meatballs (see page 102)

Braciole (see page 100)

A cooking lesson with my son Neil and me.

I don't know why we've always called our meat sauce "gravy," but we have as long as I can remember. Perhaps it's because with all of the delicious meats cooked into it, like different types of Italian sausages (sweet, spicy, some prepared with fennel, some with parsley, some with lots of garlic); meatballs, sometimes prepared with beef, sometimes with veal; and Braciole, it becomes so thick and rich—much more like a gravy than a sauce. Sometimes I'll even throw some ribs or pancetta (Italian bacon) into it. Each type of meat will give your sauce a completely unique and delicious flavor.

Try making a big pot of this "gravy" and freezing it in smaller containers. There's nothing like coming home from a hard day's work, and all you have to do to make a terrific meal for your family is thaw out your meats and sauce and put up a pot of pasta!

Parboil the tomatoes in a big pot of water for a few minutes to loosen their skin. Remove their skin and put the tomatoes aside.

Place the onion, garlic, and olive oil in a large pot and sauté lightly, making sure not to brown the garlic. Squash the tomatoes through a colander, tossing out the hard ends, and add the crushed tomatoes and their juice. Stir in the oregano and basil, sugar, and some salt and pepper. Cover tightly and simmer over low heat, stirring regularly. If you like a smoother sauce, you may want to blend half of this mixture in a blender and return it to the pot.

Rinse a large skillet and leave the moisture in it. Brown the sausages (they do not need to be cooked all the way through since they will finish cooking in the sauce). Add the browned sausages to the tomato mixture. Add your prepared Meatballs, your prepared Braciole rolls, and whatever other meats you wish to add to the sauce. Cover tightly and continue simmering over very low heat, periodically stirring lightly. (Be sure not to stir too briskly, because this will cause the meats to tear apart too much in the sauce.)

For best results (meaning a delicious, rich sauce!), simmer the sauce for a few hours, adjusting the salt and pepper to your taste as you cook the sauce. This recipe makes a large pot of sauce, good for a meal for at least a dozen people.

To serve, remove the meats and place them on a platter. Pour the sauce into a large dish and serve the sauce and the platter of meats along with your favorite pasta.

VEAL SAUCE

¼ cup butter
½ cup sliced mushrooms
1 cup chopped onion
½ cup chopped celery
3 cloves garlic, minced
½ cup grated carrot
1 pound ground veal
4 cups chopped tomatoes
1 teaspoon oregano
1 cup dry red wine
2 cups chicken broth
Salt and pepper to taste

Veal is a delicious meat that has a natural, spicy flavor all its own. Simmering the veal slowly with the other ingredients brings out its subtle flavor and creates a sauce that you will want to make again and again.

Melt the butter in a large skillet, and sauté the mushrooms, onion, celery, garlic, and carrot for 5 minutes.

Add the veal and sauté, stirring continuously, until the meat begins to brown. Add the chopped tomatoes, oregano, red wine, and chicken broth, stirring well. Cover tightly, and simmer over low heat for an hour, stirring periodically. About half-way through cooking the sauce, add salt and pepper to your taste.

GREEN SAUCE

1 slice Italian bread
1 cup olive oil
½ cup fresh parsley
1 tablespoon fresh basil
4 cloves garlic
½ cup fresh lemon juice
½ teaspoon sugar
½ teaspoon salt
½ teaspoon pepper
½ cup minced green bell pepper
2 tablespoons capers
½ cup thinly sliced green olives
Freshly grated Romano cheese

This is a fresh-tasting and tangy sauce that I love to use in the summer months. You can even use it in a chilled pasta salad, adding a variety of julienned vegetables.

Put the bread, olive oil, parsley, basil, garlic cloves, lemon juice, sugar, salt, and pepper in a blender, and blend well. If it's too thick, add more olive oil and lemon juice in equal amounts. Transfer this to a small saucepan.

Stir in the green pepper, capers, and green olives. Heat the sauce but do not boil. Toss the sauce into your favorite freshly made pasta. Adjust the salt and pepper to your taste.

SWEET CORN SAUCE

6 large ears fresh corn
¼ cup olive oil
1 large green bell pepper, diced
1 large red bell pepper, diced
1 medium onion, diced
4 large cloves garlic, minced
½ tablespoon oregano
½ tablespoon basil
1 ½ cups half & half
Salt and pepper to taste

This will be an unusual sauce to many who read this book, but it's an old family recipe. It is such a fresh and delicious-tasting sauce, particularly in the summer months when you can get your best and freshest vegetables, that I am sure it will quickly become one of your family's favorites as well.

Using a sharp knife, cut the corn kernels off of each ear of corn, then cream the corn in a food processor or blender. Heat the olive oil in a large, deep skillet. Add the peppers, onion, and garlic, and sauté lightly over low heat until the vegetables are slightly tender. Add the creamed corn, oregano, and basil, then cover and simmer for about 20 minutes. Stir in the half & half and the salt and pepper to taste, and continue to simmer over very low heat for 5 minutes. (Be sure not to boil or else the cream will coagulate.)

This sauce will complement just about any pasta that you put it on, but it is also delicious as a vegetable side dish all by itself.

SALSA BIANCA
WHITE SAUCE

1 large onion, minced

2 ounces butter

2 cups chicken broth

1/2 cup dry white wine

2 egg yolks, beaten

2 tablespoons lemon juice

1 heaping tablespoon minced fresh
  parsley

Salt and pepper to taste

This is a popular sauce in my neighborhood and goes well with just about any grilled or poached fish. It's terrific with clams and pasta too.

In a medium-size skillet, sauté the onion in one half of the butter until the onion is clear but not browned. Add the chicken broth and wine, and bring to a boil. Add the remaining butter, and stir until it is melted and blended well with the mixture. Whisk in the egg yolks briskly so that they blend into the sauce without separating. Remove from the heat and quickly whisk in the lemon juice, making sure that the sauce doesn't curdle. Stir in the parsley and the salt and pepper to taste.

PESTO ALLA GENOVESE E CREMA DI BASILICO
OLD WORLD PESTO SAUCE

1/2 cup chopped fresh basil

2 tablespoons pine nuts

4 tablespoons grated Romano cheese

4 large garlic cloves

1 cup olive oil

1 teaspoon coarsely chopped fresh
  parsley

1/2 teaspoon salt

Half & half (optional)

Mammanon used to make pesto the old-fashioned way—with a mortar. First she would pound and grind the herbs, nuts, and garlic, then she would gradually add the olive oil to make a smooth paste. When I was young, I used to do it this way too. Try the method below—it works just as well.

Combine all of the ingredients in a blender and blend until very smooth.

Makes enough sauce for 1 pound of pasta.

There are two ways I serve a pesto sauce on my pasta. The first and the more traditional way is in a large serving bowl that I've heated in the oven. I toss in the pesto with a generous lump of butter, and after the butter has melted, I toss my pasta in and stir the sauce into it. I almost always serve this along with a bowl of freshly grated Romano cheese—absolutely scrumptious!

CREAMY PESTO SAUCE
Some of my family favor this. I heat the pesto in a small saucepan until it is very hot but not sticking to the pan yet, and gradually stir in some half & half. (Be sure not to bring this to a boil or it will curdle.) Then toss this creamy sauce into your pasta and serve.

SALSA DI CAROTE PICCANTE
SPICY CARROT SAUCE

3 pounds carrots, peeled and sliced

1/4 cup olive oil

1 cup chopped onions

1/4 cup minced garlic

1/2 teaspoon crushed hot red peppers

1 tablespoon fresh oregano

1 tablespoon sweet basil

1/2 cup dry red wine

1 teaspoon salt

2 pounds spicy Italian sausages,
  sliced

My mother always told me that before tomatoes were "invented" in Italy, our ancestors made this sauce. I found out later that tomatoes weren't always a part of Italian culture and cooking but were imported to Italy at some time in Italy's history. I know that you'll like this delicious and wholesome sauce.

Bring a pot of water to a boil and cook the carrots until they are tender. Transfer the carrots to a blender or food processor, and purée them. Simmer this in a large pot, covered, over low heat. (Add some of the water the carrots were cooked in if the sauce is too thick.)

Heat the olive oil in a skillet, and sauté the onion, garlic, and red peppers until the onion is clear, making sure not to brown. Add this mixture to the carrot purée, as well as the oregano, basil, red wine, and salt.

Sauté the sausages in a large skillet until lightly browned. Transfer them to the sauce, cover tightly, and continue simmering over low heat for 30 to 45 minutes, stirring regularly. Adjust seasoning. Add as much of the carrot water as you need to achieve the proper consistency.

NOTE: The sausages give the sauce such a deliciously rich quality that I almost always use them in my carrot sauce. However, for your vegetarian friends, you could omit the sausages.

MARINARA SAUCE

Although a good marinara sauce is best when simmered for at least an hour or two, you actually can make one that is tasty in just 20 minutes. Blend your tomatoes in a high-speed blender for a few minutes, and rapid-boil them with the rest of the ingredients, and you will have a delicious, what I call, "quick sauce."

$\frac{1}{8}$ cup minced garlic
3 tablespoons olive oil
5 pounds ripe plum or regular
    tomatoes
1 cup dry red wine (optional)
1 tablespoon oregano
1 tablespoon basil
1 teaspoon thyme
1 pinch rosemary
Salt and pepper to taste

Lightly sauté the garlic in the olive oil in a large pot for a few minutes. Be careful not to brown the garlic. Remove pan from heat.

In another large pot, steam the tomatoes until soft, reserving the liquid. Remove the skins, and squash the tomatoes through a colander, removing the hard stem ends. (If you use canned tomatoes, do not steam them beforehand.) Put the tomatoes and their juice, red wine (if you choose), and the steaming liquid into the pot with the garlic. Add the oregano, basil, thyme, and rosemary. Season with salt and pepper. (If the tomatoes are not juicy, and depending on how long you cook your sauce, you can add some water. You want your sauce thinner than a meat sauce but not too watery either.)

Bring the sauce to a boil and then turn the heat down low. Cover tightly, and simmer for an hour or two, stirring regularly.

SPICY MARINARA SAUCE

1 large onion, minced
$\frac{1}{8}$ cup minced garlic
2 tablespoons minced red, green, or
    yellow hot peppers
2 tablespoons olive oil
1 cup chopped carrots
5 pounds ripe plum or regular tomatoes
1 cup dry red wine (optional)
1 tablespoon oregano
1 tablespoon basil
1 teaspoon thyme
1 pinch rosemary
1 cup tomato paste
Salt and pepper to taste

I make this sauce for some of my seafood dishes, but it can be used in many other ways. Serve it with pasta, with various meats, with chicken—with any dish that you need a nice marinara for. I like to add chopped carrots because their sweetness helps get rid of some of the acidity from the tomato paste.

In a large pot, lightly sauté the onion, garlic, and hot peppers in the olive oil, being careful not to brown any of the vegetables. Add the chopped carrots. In another large pot, steam the tomatoes until soft, reserving the liquid. Remove the skins, and squash the tomatoes

through a colander, removing the hard stem ends. (If you use canned tomatoes, you do not need to steam them beforehand.) Add the tomatoes and their juice, along with the steaming liquid and red wine (if you choose) to the onion mixture. Stir in the oregano, basil, thyme, rosemary, and salt and pepper to taste. Stir in the tomato paste in order to thicken the sauce. Bring the sauce to a boil, cover, and then turn the heat down low. Simmer for about an hour or two, stirring regularly.

NOTE: Be sure to wear rubber gloves when mincing the hot peppers. They will burn your skin if they are the real thing!

SALSA D'ACCIUGHE AL MARSALA
ANCHOVY SAUCE WITH MARSALA

2 cups thinly sliced mushrooms
$^{1}/_{2}$ cup minced onion
$^{1}/_{8}$ cup minced garlic
$^{3}/_{4}$ cup chopped anchovies
2 tablespoons butter
2 tablespoons olive oil
2 cups chicken broth
$^{1}/_{2}$ cup Marsala wine
1 teaspoon mustard
1/4 teaspoon cayenne pepper
2 tablespoons capers
Salt to taste

This sauce is especially good on just about any variety of grilled fish or meat—and, of course, on just about any pasta as well!

In a large skillet, sauté the mushrooms, onion, garlic, and anchovies in the butter and olive oil, being careful not to brown them. When they're tender, add the broth, wine, and mustard. Simmer over very low heat for 5 to 10 minutes. Stir in the cayenne and capers, and season with salt to taste.

DOLCI
DESSERTS

We Italians are proud of our desserts—and, like many of our foods, they have a long history. It was the traders of Venice who got Italians started on dessert making. When they set sail for the East, as far back as the Middle Ages, they brought sugar home with them. It didn't take Italian cooks long to learn what to do with the sugar—and that is how the art of making *I dolci*, or sweets, began. Dessert making spread from Italy to the rest of Europe, but in Italy, the home of European desserts, we are still famous for our pastries and sweets.

In our family, we bring our best desserts out on the feast days—on Sunday, at Christmas and Easter, at weddings and other special occasions. Those are the times to really make a show with sweets. And, at those special times, dessert is not just one dish, but it is an assortment of delicious and rich dishes that everyone will love and remember. Then, you serve fruit and nuts—that's the final course of a traditional Italian meal.

Some of the recipes I have included here are very traditional—like Baba au Rum and Cannoli. Even though you can find Cannoli in your local Italian bakery, if you want them to be the very best, you have to make them yourself! Other recipes in this section are our family favorites—like Pesche al Vino Rosso (Peaches in Red Wine Sauce), which Mammanon made because Poppanon loved peaches so much. Or Fichi alla Panico (Figs Panico), a dish made with figs, Irish Cream, walnuts, and pecans, which my son Neil invented because he loves figs so much.

Some of the recipes are traditional dishes with a new twist—like my "melt in your mouth" Frittelle di Castagne (Chestnut Fritters) and my "can't eat them fast enough" Zeppole (Sweet Puffs). My recipe for traditional Budino di Riso (Rice Pudding) is also included, but it has some surprises: The pudding is rich with figs and Ricotta cheese.

With desserts, you want everything to taste scrumptious—that is why, even in recipes that sound simple (Ricotta Cheese Pie, for example) you will find walnuts, pine nuts, orange peel, and brandy included—they make the dish unforgettable.

Because we serve them only once in a while, our desserts can be as rich and delicious as you can make them. Since nobody needs to feel guilty about these occasional pleasures, go ahead. Enjoy, enjoy!

My approach to cooking for my family is what we Italians call "abundanza"—abundance!

ITALIAN CHEESE CAKE

2 cups all-purpose flour

$^{1}/_{4}$ teaspoon salt

$^{1}/_{2}$ cup butter

1 cup ground walnuts

1 tablespoon brown sugar

2 tablespoons cooking sherry

6 tablespoons water

3 pounds Ricotta cheese

1 teaspoon vanilla

1 tablespoon baking powder

8 eggs

1 $^{1}/_{2}$ cups sugar

$^{1}/_{4}$ cup grated lemon peel

Mammanon always called her cheese cake "Sweet Pie," and to this day our family still calls it that. There are a variety of crusts that work well with an Italian cheese cake. The one below is my favorite. I've also included some delicious alternatives.

Preheat the oven to 350°F.

Sift the flour and the salt together. Using a pastry cutter, cut in the butter until the flour mixture has achieved a mealy consistency. Add the walnuts and brown sugar, and mix thoroughly. Add the sherry and the water, and form into a large, smooth ball. (You may have to add a small amount of extra water in

order to achieve this.) Chill in the refrigerator for about 30 minutes.

On a floured pastry board, roll the crust into a thin, oblong shape. Press into a large glass baking dish and set aside.

Combine the cheese, vanilla, baking powder, eggs, sugar, and lemon peel in a large mixing bowl and whip with electric beaters until smooth. Pour the filling into the crust and smooth out with a knife. Bake for 1 1/2 hours, or until the top of the pie is golden. Be sure not to overbake this pie or it will be too dry.   *Serves 8.*

VARIATIONS

1. You can change the flavor of the cheese cake by omitting the lemon peel and using any of the following flavors instead: orange peel, cinnamon, anisette (try flavoring your crust with this as well as your filling), or grated semi-sweet chocolate.

2. Use the Struffoli dough (see page 176). for a sweet, flaky crust. Roll out the dough thin and oblong, shape it into the baking dish, and proceed as above.

3. For a Zwieback crust combine 3 cups ground Zwieback crumbs with 3/4 cup brown sugar and 1/2 cup melted butter. Press this mixture into the baking dish bottom and sides, reserving some of it to sprinkle on top of the pie as well. Bake the same as above.

Two of my neighbor's children out on the firescape in Brooklyn.

FICHI ALLA PANICO
FIGS PANICO

Many of the Italian families in our neighborhood grow fig trees in their small backyards. It's one of our traditions, like growing fresh basil, a part of our Italian heritage.

Fresh, ripe figs are absolutely delicious all by themselves, but my son Neil invented this recipe because he is a gourmet cook and he loves figs. And to tell you the truth, I'd give him an award for this one.

$\frac{1}{2}$ cup coarsely chopped walnuts
$\frac{1}{2}$ cup coarsely chopped pecans
1 pound ripe and soft fresh figs
$\frac{1}{2}$ cup half & half
1 cup Irish Cream

Preheat the oven to 375°F.

Bake the walnuts and pecans on a baking sheet until lightly toasted, approximately 10 minutes. Let cool.

Wash the figs well in cold water, cut into bite-size wedges, and place in a mixing bowl. Mix in the toasted nuts.

In another mixing bowl, beat the half & half and Irish Cream until frothy. Fold into the figs. Chill for at least an hour before serving.   *Serves 4.*

My son Neil with his first love, Rosemary, on her birthday in 1952. That's Rosemary's cousin Joan with them.

RICE PUDDING

2 cups uncooked rice

Vegetable oil

8 eggs

1 ½ cups sugar

1 tablespoon vanilla

2 pounds Ricotta cheese

1 can evaporated milk
   or 1 pint half & half

1 ½ teaspoons cinnamon

1 ½ cups chopped dried figs

The secret to this recipe, or any rice dish for that matter, is to cook the rice in such a way that it is soft and fluffy, not sticky. Mammanon taught me to make rice the way that I've described in this recipe. It may take you a few times to get it right—it did me. But once you master it, you will have a perfectly light and delicious rice every time you make it.

In a large saucepan, sauté the rice lightly in just enough vegetable oil to coat it. Be sure not to brown it. Cover the hot rice with about an inch of water above the rice. Bring this to a boil, cover, and turn down the heat very low. Simmer for about 15 to 20 minutes. (Do not take off the cover while the rice is cooking! The steam is what really cooks the rice the best and makes it come out fluffy.)

Preheat the oven to 350°F.

In a large mixing bowl, beat the eggs, sugar, vanilla, Ricotta cheese, evaporated milk, and cinnamon until smooth and creamy. Stir in the rice and the figs, and pour into a lightly buttered, oblong cake pan (glass or stainless steel). Bake for about 45 minutes, or until the top is golden brown. (Be sure not to over-bake or the pudding will be too dry.)

Remove the dish from the oven and let it cool and settle for a few minutes before serving. (Some people like to serve this dessert piping hot, straight from the oven, and some prefer to chill it first.) Serve in dessert dishes topped with some sweetened whipped cream.

Serves 6 to 8.

VARIATION

BREAD PUDDING: Cut a loaf of dry, hardened Italian Bread into small squares and add it to the Ricotta/egg mixture in place of the rice. Let soak well until bread softens, about 5 minutes. Add the dried fig pieces, and proceed as above.

These cookies are my family's all-time favorite dessert to serve at the end of a meal, along with espresso or coffee. You can go into any bakery in my neighborhood and see piles and piles of them in every shape, color, and flavor. They're so simple to make that I always have a large tin of them on hand at home to serve to family and friends.

I know the recipes on this page seem very similar to each other, but I have kept them that way because that is how I got them from my mother. I use these basic cookie recipes over and over again, but I alter them in so many ways to make them different.

For example, I use food coloring, different sprinkles, confectioners' sugar, liqueurs, vanilla, almond, orange, and lemon flavorings, as well as a variety of chopped nuts and seeds to change the colors and flavors. The other thing I do is prepare a basic white icing to ice the butter cookies, then color and/or flavor the icing in different ways. I also make the cookies in many shapes and sizes, using either my cookie press or cookie cutter shapes that I've collected over the years. You can prepare the cookie dough ahead of time, freeze it, and use it any time you wish. Save time and please your family and friends—now that's my idea of a good recipe!

BISCOTTINI DA TÈ
BUTTER COOKIES

½ cup shortening
½ cup butter
2 cups sugar
4 eggs, beaten
3 teaspoons vanilla
3 cups all-purpose flour
2 teaspoons baking powder
1 teaspoons salt

In a large mixing bowl, cream the shortening, butter, and sugar. Add the eggs and vanilla, then blend in the flour, baking powder, and salt. Chill for 1 to 2 hours.

Preheat the oven to 350°F.

Roll out the chilled dough and cut into shapes with a cookie cutter. (I prefer to use the old cookie press that belonged to my mother.) Bake the cookies on a greased cookie sheet until they're a light golden brown, about 8 to 10 minutes. Transfer to racks to cool. *Makes 3 dozen cookies.*

NOTE: At Christmas, you can cover the cookies with green and red sprinkles or sprinkle confectioners' sugar over them while the cookies are still slightly warm. At Easter, cover them with pastels.

QUARESIMALI GRECI
GREEK EASTER COOKIES

½ cup butter
1 cup margarine
2 cups sugar
3 eggs
1 cup milk
2 tablespoons vanilla
3 teaspoons baking powder
½ teaspoons baking soda

4 cups flour
Confectioners' sugar for dusting cookies

Preheat the oven to 350°F.

Cream the butter and margarine with the sugar in a large mixing bowl. Mix the eggs into this mixture, then beat in the milk, vanilla, baking powder, and baking soda.

Gradually stir in the flour, creating a firm cookie dough.

Using a cookie press, press out the various shapes onto an ungreased cookie sheet. Bake until they're golden, 12 to 15 minutes. Dust lightly with confectioners' sugar while the cookies are still slightly warm.
Makes 3 dozen cookies.

ANICI
SEEDED ANISETTE COOKIES

4 cups flour
3 teaspoons baking powder
¾ cup sugar
½ cup canola oil
3 eggs
3 teaspoons anisette
Hulled sesame seeds
Flour for working cookie dough

Sift the flour and baking powder together in a mixing bowl and set aside. Beat the sugar and oil together in another mixing bowl. Add the eggs and anisette, and whip. Gradually beat in the flour and baking powder mixture.

Preheat the oven to 375°F.

Roll out onto a floured baking board and form into a cookie roll, about 1 1/2 to 2 inches wide. Sprinkle the sesame seeds liberally onto a clean dish towel. (If you can find them, the sweetened sesame seeds work well. If not, the plain are fine.) Roll the cookie roll all over and into the seeds until the cookie roll is well coated and embedded with the seeds.

Place the cookie roll back onto the floured baking board and slice into cookies about 1 1/2 inches deep. Arrange the cookies on an ungreased cookie sheet and bake for 12 to 15 minutes, until they're golden brown.
Makes 3 dozen cookies.

GENOVESE RUM CAKE

CAKE

1 ¼ cups all-purpose flour
¼ teaspoon salt
8 eggs, separated
2 tablespoons dark rum
1 ¼ cups sugar
2 tablespoons grated orange rind

This is a very light and beautiful cake. Each bite melts in your mouth.

Preheat the oven to 350°F. Sift the flour and salt together. In a separate mixing bowl, beat the egg yolks and rum, then gradually beat in 3/4 cup of the sugar until the mixture is light and fluffy. Fold in the flour mixture and the orange rind.

Beat the egg whites until they peak. Gradually beat in the rest of the sugar. Fold this into the flour mixture. Turn into an ungreased, 9-inch pan. Bake for 30 minutes, or until the cake is golden and has begun to come away from the sides of the pan. Remove from the pan, and place on a cake rack to cool completely.

RUM CREAM FILLING AND ICING

1 ½ pints whipping cream
1 ¼ cups confectioners' sugar
½ cup dark rum
Cocoa for dusting

In a mixing bowl, whip the cream until stiff. Beat in the sugar, then the rum. When the cake has cooled, spread the whipped cream evenly over the top and sides. Sift some cocoa over the top.

Makes one 9-inch cake.

RICOTTA CHEESE PIE

2 cups + 1 tablespoon flour
1 teaspoon baking powder
¼ teaspoon salt
¾ cup butter
3 tablespoons brandy
1 ½ pounds Ricotta cheese
2 tablespoons grated orange peel
½ cup chopped walnuts
½ cup pine nuts
4 eggs
1 cup sugar
2 teaspoons vanilla
Confectioners' sugar for garnishing

This is a hearty, thick, and nourishing cheese cake, with an unusual blend of flavors and textures.

Sift 2 cups of the flour, the baking powder, and the salt together in a large bowl. Using a pastry cutter, cut in the butter until the flour beads up. Add the brandy gradually, and work the dough into a firm ball. Chill for an hour, covered with a cloth.

Roll three quarters of the dough to at least 1/8-inch thickness. If you prefer, you can do this between two sheets of waxed paper (this helps prevent sticking). Butter a 9-inch pie pan (this helps brown the bottom of the pie), and press your crust into the pan.

Preheat the oven to 375°F.

In a mixing bowl, beat the cheese, remaining flour, orange peel, and nuts. In another mixing bowl, whip the eggs until they are frothy and light, and gradually beat in the sugar and vanilla. Fold the egg mixture into the cheese mixture, and pour into the pie pan.

Roll out the remaining pie dough. Cut the dough into strips and arrange in a lattice design across the pie. Bake until the filling is firm and the crust is golden brown, approximately 40 minutes. You may want to use a pastry brush to brush some egg white over the top and along the edges of the crust. This gives the crust a beautiful sheen and makes it look mouth watering! Cool before serving and sprinkle liberally with confectioners' sugar.

Serves 6 to 8.

NEAPOLITAN HONEY BALLS

Struffoli is a light and crispy dessert, and one of the most popular desserts in my culture. You can find them in every Italian bakery around me, and they're perfect to nibble on with friends over a cup of espresso.

4 cups flour
1 cup sugar
2 teaspoons baking powder
½ cup butter or vegetable shortening
2 teaspoons vanilla
6 large eggs
Vegetable oil for deep frying
Honey for coating the balls

Blend the flour, sugar, and baking powder in a large mixing bowl. Mix in the shortening or butter with a pastry blender or a fork, then blend in the vanilla and the eggs, two at a time. The batter should be like a very thick cookie dough. Knead the dough for 5 minutes, until very smooth. Flour your hands when the dough gets sticky. Place the dough on your floured baking board, and form it into a large ball. Dust the dough lightly with flour, cover with a clean cloth, and let it sit for 1/2 hour.

Divide the large ball into 3 or 4 smaller balls. Roll each ball into 1/2-inch rolls. Cut each roll into 1/2-inch round pieces.

In a deep skillet, heat enough vegetable oil for deep frying. Drop the balls (about a dozen at a time) into the oil, and fry until golden and crispy. Transfer to either paper towels or a metal colander to drain.

While they are still warm, put the struffoli into a large mixing bowl. Heat the honey in a small saucepan and drizzle it over the struffoli while you gently stir them. All the struffoli should be lightly coated with the honey. Serve warm, piled in a mound on a serving platter.

VARIATIONS

1. BOWS: For very special occasions and feasts, I like to make the struffoli bows the way my mother always did. Prepare the dough as above, but instead of dividing the dough into 3 or 4 parts, roll the whole thing out into a rectangle the thickness of pie crust. Cut into strips about 1 1/2 inches wide by 10 to 12 inches long, or vary the width and length of the strips to make assorted bow sizes.

To form the bow, place 2 fingers in the middle of the strip. Spread your fingers apart and fold one end of the strip over your fingers, then the other end of the strip over your fingers and the first strip. Pinch the center together, forming the bow. Heat your oil in a deep skillet and proceed as above, using a spatula to drop the bows into the oil. Sprinkle liberally with confectioners' sugar while warm.

2. For Easter, after we coat the struffoli with honey, we usually coat them with pastel-colored sprinkles. For Christmas, we usually coat them with green and red sprinkles, or we sprinkle them with confectioners' sugar. An alternative is to stir minced citron (orange, lemon, etc.) into the honey or even drizzle the struffoli with a dark chocolate sauce. There are so many ways to create different flavors and different festive looks.

SWEET PUFFS

½ cup butter

6 tablespoons sugar

4 eggs

2 tablespoons vegetable oil

4 tablespoons brandy

½ teaspoon salt

1 tablespoon grated lemon peel

1 ½ cups flour

Vegetable shortening for deep frying

Confectioners' sugar

Zeppole is a childhood treat that my mother always made and that has always been a favorite of my kids as well. Served hot, they melt in your mouth. Your kids will eat them faster than you can make them!

Cream the butter and sugar together in a medium bowl. Mix in the eggs, oil, brandy, salt, lemon peel, and flour. Heat the shortening in a skillet, and drop teaspoons of the batter into it (any oil can be substituted). Fry several zeppole at a time over medium heat until they get puffy and golden. Drain on paper towels. Serve hot, sprinkled with confectioners' sugar.

CHESTNUT FRITTERS

2 cups chestnuts, peeled

2 cups milk

½ teaspoon salt

2 tablespoons butter

2 tablespoons sugar

1 teaspoon vanilla

5 egg yolks + 1 egg yolk, beaten

1 cup fine bread crumbs, unseasoned

Vegetable oil for frying

Confectioners' sugar

These fritters melt in your mouth, I kid you not. They're perfect for that cold, holiday evening.

Combine the chestnuts, milk, and salt in a saucepan and simmer until the chestnuts are tender. Remove from the heat, drain, and mash well. Add the butter, sugar, vanilla, the 5 egg yolks, and mix well.

Take spoonful by spoonful of the mixture and roll them into balls. Dip them in the beaten egg yolk, then roll them in the bread crumbs. Fry each fritter in hot vegetable oil until golden brown, and drain on paper towels. Serve hot, sprinkled with confectioners' sugar.

My son Neil and his friends in Atlantic City sometime in the 50s.

ITALIAN TRIFLE

1 quart milk (or half & half for
    a richer sauce)

1 teaspoon vanilla

8 teaspoons sugar

8 egg yolks

6 tablespoons flour

2 teaspoons grated lemon rind

2 tablespoons butter

1 large sponge cake or 2 dozen
    ladyfingers

6 ounces rum and 6 ounces
    maraschino, mixed together

Whipping cream

3 teaspoons confectioners' sugar

Thin lemon and orange slices

There are as many different versions of this scrumptious dessert in my neighborhood as there are dialects. This is the one Mammanon would make when she really wanted to make someone feel special. And it worked every time. One bite and everyone had a smile on their face!

Bring water to a boil in the bottom of a double boiler. In a saucepan, scald the milk with the vanilla. Blend the sugar, egg yolks, flour, and grated lemon rind in the top of the double boiler, stirring constantly. Gradually add the scalded milk, beating until the mixture is thick and smooth. Remove the top of the double boiler from the heat and beat in the butter. Set aside to cool, stirring periodically to maintain a smooth consistency and to release the steam from the pudding.

Cut the sponge cake in 1/2-inch slices (or use the ladyfingers) and soak them with the rum and maraschino mixture. Pour half of the cooled pudding into the bottom of a large glass serving bowl and smooth out. Arrange half of the liqueur-soaked cake slices on top, then cover with the rest of the pudding mixture. Arrange the rest of the liqueur-soaked cake slices on top.

Sweeten the cream with the confectioners' sugar and whip until stiff. Spread over the top of the dish. Chill for at least an hour and serve in slices. Garnish with slices of lemon and orange.   *Serves 6.*

ALMOND MACAROON COOKIES

6 egg yolks

2 cups confectioners' sugar

1/4 teaspoon salt

1 teaspoon grated orange rind

1 1/2 cups cake flour

6 egg whites

1 cup coconut

1 1/2 cups blanched and slivered
    almonds

These are very light and crunchy cookies, and perfect to keep on hand to serve an unexpected guest over for a cup of coffee.

Combine the egg yolks, sugar, salt, and orange rind in a mixing bowl and beat until thick and creamy. Stir in one half of the flour.

In another bowl, beat the egg whites until they stand up in stiff peaks. Fold one half of this into the flour mixture. Stir in the rest of the flour, then fold in the rest of the egg white and the coconut.

Preheat the oven to 350°F. Grease a baking sheet with butter, then dust with flour. Place the cookie dough into a large pastry bag and squeeze out rounds about 3 inches in diameter. Sprinkle slivered almonds over the top of each one. Bake until the cookies are delicately browned.
   Makes 2 dozen cookies.

That's my daughter Annette blowing out the candles on her cake, with some of her cousins looking on.

NEAPOLITAN RICOTTA CUPS

2 cups all-purpose flour
1/4 teaspoon salt
1/2 cup sugar
1/2 cup butter
2 egg yolks
Grated rind of 1 lemon +
    1 teaspoon
1 1/2 pounds Ricotta cheese
1 cup confectioners' sugar
2 egg yolks
1/4 teaspoon cinnamon
4 tablespoons raisins (optional)

This is a rich and delicious dessert, and one that we like to prepare often for our Sunday family dinners.

Sift the flour, salt, and sugar into a medium-size bowl. Cut in the butter with a pastry blender or a fork to distribute it evenly. Add one egg yolk at a time, mixing well after each one. Stir in the rind of 1 lemon.

Work the dough with your hands until it is soft and manageable, and it comes away easily from the sides of the bowl. If necessary, add a bit of water to hold it together. Turn the dough onto a floured board and knead quickly until smooth and pliable. Wrap the dough in waxed paper and refrigerate for 1 hour.

Roll out the dough to about 1/4 inch thick on a floured board. Using a glass or a cookie cutter, cut the pastry into rounds to fit the bottoms of muffin pans.

Preheat the oven to 350°F.

In a large mixing bowl, combine the cheese, sugar, egg yolks, cinnamon, and 1 teaspoon lemon rind. Beat with electric beaters until smooth and creamy. Stir in the raisins, if desired. Press the pastry rounds into the bottoms of the muffin pans, and place a heaping tablespoon of the filling in the center of each. Use the leftover pastry dough to cut small strips and lay crisscross over the filling. Trim the edges to fit the muffin pans, and bake for 30 to 40 minutes, until the filling is firm and the crust is golden brown. Cool and serve.   *Makes 8 to 10 pastries.*

PEACHES IN RED WINE SAUCE

6 large peaches (fresh or canned)
4 cups dry red wine
1 cup brown sugar
Whipped cream (optional)

This is a very simple dessert, and I can remember my mother making it from the time I was a little girl. I think it was my father who really got her to start making it. He often liked to end a meal with a glass of red wine. He would pull out his small knife from his vest pocket and slice off pieces of peach, dipping them in his wine before eating them. Sometimes he would let the peach slices sit in his wine for a few minutes before eating them, then finish off by drinking the wine. I think Mammanon began making this dessert for my father during the winter months, when she couldn't get fresh peaches for him!

Preheat the oven to 350°F.

Peel the peaches, and slice them into nice, thick slices. Arrange them in a liberally buttered baking dish.

Mix the wine and sugar together in a small mixing bowl, then pour over the peaches. Cover the baking dish tightly and bake for 45 minutes. Serve straight from the oven, or cooled down with some whipped cream on top.   *Serves 4.*

VARIATION
Try the same dish with pears, fresh berries, or even apples.

BABA RUM CAKES

Besides cannoli, "baba rums" are my family's favorite dessert for a special meal. Sometimes I will make a custard to put on top of them, sometimes a sweetened whipped cream, but 99 percent of the time I serve them just soaked in the rum sauce. However you do them, they are sure to be a hit.

CAKES
1 cake active yeast
1/4 cup milk, warmed
2 cups all-purpose flour
2 tablespoons sugar
1/3 teaspoon salt
4 eggs, beaten
6 tablespoons butter, melted
2/3 cup chopped seedless raisins (optional)

Dissolve the yeast in the warmed milk. Sift the flour, sugar, and salt together in a large bowl. Make a well in the center and pour the yeast and eggs into it. Add the raisins (if you choose). Using a wooden spoon, work these ingredients together into a smooth dough, adding a bit more milk if the dough seems too stiff. Work in the melted butter. Knead the dough several times, cover, and let stand in a warm place for 30 to 60 minutes. Preheat the oven to 350°F.

Divide the dough evenly into either greased tart molds or cupcake pans, filling each about three-quarters full. Bake for about 30 minutes, until the baba have risen above the top of their molds or pans and are nicely browned. Remove the cakes from their pans and let cool on cake racks.

RUM SAUCE
1/2 cup water
1 1/4 cups sugar
1 cup rum
1/2 teaspoon cinnamon (optional)
1/2 teaspoon grated lemon peel (optional)
1 teaspoon vanilla (optional)

Bring the water and sugar to a boil in a small saucepan. Turn down the heat and simmer for 15 minutes. Remove the pan from heat and add first the rum, then whatever additional flavor you choose—lemon, cinnamon, or vanilla. Dunk the cakes in the rum mixture until they are soaked. Refrigerate before serving them.

Serves 4.

CHOCOLATE COVERED MERINGUES

Meringues are a classic Italian cookie. Without the chocolate coating, they are a very light, crunchy, simple cookie, and one that I often gave to my kids when they were young. But dipped in the chocolate sauce, they are out of this world.

MERINGUE
6 egg whites
1 cup sugar
Pinch salt

Preheat the oven to 250°F.

In a mixing bowl, beat the egg whites with the sugar and salt, adding the sugar gradually. Beat until the egg whites are stiff. Either put the meringue in a pastry bag and form into small circles (about 2 inches across), or form with a spoon. Bake the meringues on a buttered cookie sheet for about 15 to 20 minutes, or until they're a light golden brown. Set them aside to cool.

CHOCOLATE SAUCE
1/2 cup half & half
1 teaspoon vanilla
1/2 cup sugar
4 egg yolks, beaten
4 ounces semi-sweet chocolate, grated
Confectioners' sugar

Heat the half & half in the top of a double boiler. Stir in the vanilla, then the sugar. Whisk in the beaten egg yolks gradually and add the semi-sweet chocolate, stirring constantly until the sauce thickens.

Remove the pan from the heat and allow the sauce to cool, stirring frequently. Dip the tops of the cooled meringues in the sauce, lay them on waxed paper, and let the chocolate harden. Sprinkle them with confectioners' sugar.

CANNOLI

This is the most basic dessert that we serve. Every bakery in our neighborhood makes them—so much so, that I rarely prepare them myself anymore! (My daughter-in-law loves them so much, that I do make an exception when she comes to Brooklyn.) For every Italian dialect, you will find a slightly different variation of cannoli. Below is the style that I learned from my mother, but I've included some variations that I've seen many of my Italian neighbors use.

SHELLS

2 cups flour
2 tablespoons margarine
1 teaspoon sugar
¼ teaspoon salt
¾ cup Marsala wine
Vegetable oil for frying shells
Confectioners' sugar for dusting

To make cannoli shells, you first need to be sure you have something to shape them around. Cannoli tubes are made of a very light cookie-cutter-type tin, and are about 7 inches long and 1 1/8 inches in diameter.

Combine the flour, margarine, sugar, and salt, gradually adding the wine and blending well. Knead the dough until a rather hard paste is formed. Cut the dough in half and roll each half into a thin sheet, about 1/8 inch thick. Cut into

4 inch squares, and wrap each square around the cannoli form diagonally, overlapping the two points. Seal the points with a little dab of egg white.

Meanwhile, heat some vegetable oil in a large, deep frying pan. Drop a few of the tubes at a time into the hot oil and fry the shells on all sides until they are golden brown. Transfer them to paper towels to drain and cool, then gently remove the shells from their tubes. Repeat procedure until all the shells are made.

FILLING

1 ½ pounds Ricotta cheese
1 cup confectioners' sugar
¼ teaspoon cinnamon
¼ teaspoon vanilla

Whip all of the ingredients until smooth and creamy. Fold in any of the following ingredients to suit your taste: chopped fruit peel (orange or lemon), minced pistachio nuts, cocoa powder (or grated semi-sweet chocolate), chopped glacé cherries, minced fruit-flavored citron, or even different colored sprinkles. Adding any of these ingredients will create a completely different-flavored cannoli.

Chill the filling, then place it in a large pastry bag. Fill the cannoli shells, smoothing out the ends. Sprinkle them with confectioners' sugar and refrigerate until you are ready to serve them.

Whatever you do, don't be like my daughter-in-law and eat them for breakfast. Cannoli are meant to be served as a dessert with espresso— and that's it!

That's me in my Confirmation veil, with my prayer book and rosary. My aunt Anne is sitting with me.

POLENTA SOUFFLÉ

This is an Old World dessert, combining some very unusual flavors. Don't forget the Maraschino Sauce on top—it's scrumptious!

SOUFFLE

¼ cup finely ground polenta
2 ½ cups milk
2 tablespoons butter
6 large eggs, separated
¼ cup sugar
¼ teaspoon salt
½ cup blanched and chopped almonds
4 drops almond extract
2 ounces seedless raisins
Confectioners' sugar for dusting

Combine the polenta and the milk in the top of a double boiler. Cook until thick, stirring often with a whisk so that the polenta doesn't stick. Stir in the butter and set aside to cool.

Preheat the oven to 350°F. When the polenta has cooled somewhat, beat in the egg yolks, sugar, and salt until smooth. Stir in the almonds, almond extract, and raisins. Beat the egg whites until they form stiff peaks, and fold into the polenta mixture.

Pour the mixture into a buttered baking dish and bake for 40 to 45 minutes, until the soufflé is fluffy and golden brown. Remove from the oven, and let cool for a few minutes. With a knife, loosen the edges of the soufflé all around the baking dish. Transfer the soufflé to a serving platter and dust lightly with confectioners' sugar.

MARASCHINO SAUCE

1 cup whipping cream
2 tablespoons maraschino
¼ cup confectioners' sugar

In a mixing bowl, beat the whipping cream until fluffy. Add the maraschino and the sugar, and continue beating until the cream is stiff and forms peaks. Serve the soufflé topped with the sauce.

NEAPOLITAN APRICOT BARS

Apricot is the flavor of jam we traditionally use in this cookie recipe, but you can also use strawberry, blackberry, or other flavors to create a variety of different flavored cookies.

PASTRY

2 cups all-purpose flour
⅔ cup confectioners' sugar
⅔ cup softened butter
2 eggs
½ teaspoon almond extract
⅓ cup almond slivers
2 cups apricot jam

Sift the flour and sugar together in a large bowl. Stir in the butter, eggs, and almond extract, then work in the almond slivers. Form into a smooth ball, and refrigerate covered for 1 to 2 hours.

Preheat the oven to 350°F. Roll out the dough to form a rectangle about 1/4 inch thick. Cut into 4-inch squares and bake for 12 to 15 minutes, until they're a light golden brown. Allow cookies to cool slightly, then cut each square into 3 strips.

In a small saucepan, heat the apricot jam over low heat until the jam melts. Spread the jam over all the cookie strips, then stack the strips 3 high. Let the stacks sit and continue to cool, so that the jam dries.

ICING

2 cups confectioners' sugar
1 teaspoon vanilla
3 tablespoons boiling water

Beat the sugar, vanilla, and hot water together in a small mixing bowl. After the cookies have sat for a while, drizzle the icing over them. Serve when the icing has hardened.

ITALIAN CUSTARD

7 eggs
3 tablespoons sherry
½ cup sugar
1 tablespoon gelatin
3 tablespoons brandy
1 teaspoon grated lemon peel
Large bowl ice cubes
1 cup whipping cream, whipped
 until stiff
Lemon slices for garnish

A very simple and light pudding—and a wonderful dessert to make in a pinch when someone special stops by. I like to serve it with some of my Butter Cookies (see page 172), which I always keep on hand.

Beat the eggs in the top of a double boiler. (The water below should be at a full boil.) Add the sherry and sugar, and beat constantly. Dissolve the gelatin in the brandy and add to the mixture, along with the lemon peel. Beat continuously for 5 to 8 minutes until the mixture becomes creamy and begins to thicken.

Place the top of the double boiler in the center of a deep bowl of ice cubes. Stir the mixture until it is thick, cool, and smooth. Fold in the whipped cream and turn into individual-size parfait cups. Refrigerate before serving. Garnish with thin lemon slices.   *Serves 4.*

RECIPE NOTES

RECIPE INDEX